Poems From The Eastern Counties

Edited by Steve Twelvetree

YoungWriters
First published in Great Britain in 2005 by:
Young Writers
Remus House
Coltsfoot Drive
Peterborough
PE2 9JX
Telephone: 01733 890066
Website: www.youngwriters.co.uk

SB ISBN 1 84460 683 X

Foreword

Young Writers was established in 1991 and has been passionately devoted to the promotion of reading and writing in children and young adults ever since. The quest continues today. Young Writers remains as committed to engendering the fostering of burgeoning poetic and literary talent as ever.

This year's Young Writers competition has proven as vibrant and dynamic as ever and we are delighted to present a showcase of the best poetry from across the UK. Each poem has been carefully selected from a wealth of *Once Upon A Rhyme* entries before ultimately being published in this, our twelfth primary school poetry series.

Once again, we have been supremely impressed by the overall high quality of the entries we have received. The imagination, energy and creativity which has gone into each young writer's entry made choosing the best poems a challenging and often difficult but ultimately hugely rewarding task - the general high standard of the work submitted amply vindicating this opportunity to bring their poetry to a larger appreciative audience.

We sincerely hope you are pleased with our final selection and that you will enjoy *Once Upon A Rhyme Poems From The Eastern Counties* for many years to come.

Contents

The Poems

In My Nightmare

In my nightmare I saw
A deep red pile of flesh,
That was once a man,
Sitting in the corner of a deserted house,
Just rotting away.

In my nightmare I heard
A blood-curdling scream,
And then the sound of a gun being shot.

In my nightmare I thought
I had been put in a coffin,
And was being buried alive.

In my nightmare I saw
A great hooded beast,
Carrying an axe dripping with blood.

In my nightmare I heard
A cracking of bones,
And then the distant clodding of footsteps.

Ben Peacock (11)

Badger

Badger, black and white,
Sett, full of tunnels,
Nocturnal, vicious, energetic,
Fur like midnight sky,
Sneaky as a thief,
The old wise man of the forest
Or exterminator of the undergrowth?
Badger, black and white,
Friend or foe?

Louis Michalski (10)
Dundale Primary School, Tring

The Great White Shark

The great white shark
In the deep blue sea
Killer, corrupting, creeping
Elegant as seaweed drifting through the water
Scary as roaring thunder
Just thinking about it makes me shiver
Cold as the icy winter
The great white shark
Colossal predator of the sea.

Lauren Mayo (10)
Dundale Primary School, Tring

The Rabbit

The rabbit
Lives in warrens in the soft soil.
Eyes as huge as a second moon in the sky
Soft as a sheep
Camouflaged like a grain of sand in the desert.
It makes me happy
Warm as a sun burning in the sky.
The rabbit
Reminds me how long our life is.

Holly Bilcock (9)
Dundale Primary School, Tring

The Tibetan Terrier

The Tibetan terrier
Living in a high table land.
Furry, soft, intelligent.
Elegant as a swan swimming across a lake.
Like a star wandering in the sky.
It makes me feel warm
Like a fire glowing in the night.
The Tibetan terrier.
A perfect pet to have.

Charlotte Johnston (9)
Dundale Primary School, Tring

The Jaguar

The jaguar.
A big cat.
Maneater, powerful, camouflaged.
Streaking like a shooting star.
It makes me feel scared
Like a mouse about to die.
The jaguar.
A pet not to have.

Charlotte Colebrook (9)
Dundale Primary School, Tring

Black-Collared Lizards

Black-collared lizard
Dancing in the desert
Broad head, large mouth, narrow neck
Dark as a bottomless hole
Bumpy as a pile of rocks.
I feel powerful
As if I could control it.
Black-collared lizard
Gloomy as the night sky.

Callum Bentley (10)
Dundale Primary School, Tring

The Tiger

The tiger
Living in the jungle
Stripy, fierce, fiery
Like a thundering storm roaring through the sky
Beaming eyes like fire.
It makes me feel scared
Like a little mouse.
The tiger
Hunted by men.

Leigh Eggleton (10)
Dundale Primary School, Tring

Homework

Homework
The most evil thing known to man,
Boring, hated, mindless
Like a deadly snake ready to strike
Like torture three times a week
It makes me feel like I want to burn it
Like I want to steal the answer book
And rip it up into tiny little pieces
Homework
The thing nightmares are made of.

Jack Easton (10)
Dundale Primary School, Tring

The Rose

The rose,
One of the most beautiful flowers on Earth,
Elegant, attractive, colourful.
Like the flower of love,
Like the king of flowers,
It makes me feel joyful,
Like lightning of happiness.
The rose,
It makes me think of Grandma.

Leah Dobbs (9)
Dundale Primary School, Tring

The Runaway Bride

Maria the bride walks down the aisle,
Did she want to wait for a while?

She breathes for a bit, then looks at the floor,
Then turns around and heads for the door.

She sees the man she wanted to marry,
Then looks back and decides to tarry.

'Run, I must run,' says the nervous bride,
As she views from the seashore the raging tide.

She goes for a swim, it starts to rain,
Then she's drowning and crippled by her inner pain.

Maria is in a coffin, she has died,
Now no one will know why she's the
Runaway bride.

Sasha Challenor (10)
Ecton Primary School, Northampton

Candyfloss And Pancakes

Candyfloss, pink, spinning round and round,
Candyfloss, white, bouncing up and down.
Candyfloss, blue, count them, one, two, three,
Candyfloss on a stick, I think that one's for me!

Pancakes, thin, eat them with a fork,
Pancakes and sausages, my favourite is pork,
Pancakes, sweet taste rolling on my tongue,
Oh dear, I've forgotten to leave some for Mum!

Ella Sidey (8)
Ecton Primary School, Northampton

Autumn Is . . .

When you're walking through a forest,
Listening to some squirrels,
Eating juicy berries,
Watching leaves quiver.

When you're walking up a hillside,
Listening to some sheep,
Eating sweet apples,
Watching hungry geese.

When you're strolling through a village,
Listening to some birds,
Feeling gusts of wind,
Watching swaying pines.

Colours of leaves from red to green,
This is autumn.

Jenny Wilde (10)
Ecton Primary School, Northampton

Autumn Winds

Autumn winds blow hard and soft,
Some are bad, some are not.
Some make leaves fall off the trees,
Some just make a little breeze.

Autumn winds blow hard and soft,
Stay inside and watch the leaves
Being picked up by the breeze.

Autumn winds blow hard and soft,
As the conkers and acorns all fall down,
There is a lovely autumn breeze
In the air of all the leaves.

Casie Wright (9)
Ecton Primary School, Northampton

The Cyclist

Her hair is flying as if she is going to take off into the clouds.
She is determined to get to her destination
And her legs are golden as if she has flowing into the sun.
Her body is leaning forward
And her eyes are like a hawk
Seeking everything that's in front of her.
Her shoulders lean forward, pushing against the wind
And her hands are clenched and clutch the handlebar firmly.
Her face, deadly serious, because she wants to win the race.
Her feet and toes are slamming down on the pedals
As she crosses the finish line with joy and tears.

Lajor Cole Etti (10)
Gaddesden Row JMI School, Hemel Hempstead

The Climber

White chalk-like snow covers his fingers.
Sweat dribbles down his head.
Eyes are determined to reach the top.
Muscley, sweat-covered arms gleam in the sun.
Strong, bent legs push, impatient to finish.
He grips on to the shackle with his clenched teeth
And clips it on to the rope.
He scrambles to the top, excited and happy.
Then, clutching the rope, he swings back into the air
And abseils down to the ground.

Ellen Holdsworth (9)
Gaddesden Row JMI School, Hemel Hempstead

The Tennis Player

Her legs are tightened as she hits the ball.
She is concentrating and not putting her mind off the game.
Her hands clench around the tennis racquet.
Eyes are determined.
She will never take them off the ball.
She strikes the ball - not that hard, not that weak.
Her lips are dry.
She's stretching for the ball with every ounce of strength left.
She sweats.
She hits and . . .
She wins. She is ecstatic.

Latir Cole Etti (10)
Gaddesden Row JMI School, Hemel Hempstead

The Jockey

His head is far down, nearly touching the horse.
His face, dead straight, looking at the finish line.
His eyes are big and bold as he looks at the other racers.
His body is curled up like a hedgehog.
His back is crouched.
His arms straight like a pencil.
His bottom is up in the air bobbing up and down.
His feet kicking hard at the horse.
He reaches the finish line and he won first place by a metre.
His horse is exhausted.

Lily Highfield (10)
Gaddesden Row JMI School, Hemel Hempstead

The Skier

As she starts she turns the sharp corner.
Her hair blows back in the cold wind.
With eyes concentrating on the path before her,
Her legs bend forward to balance her.
Her hair blows in the wind
As she swerves round the second corner,
Determined to win the race.
She grips the sticks, pushing harder and harder.
The helmet is on securely
So it doesn't fall off at this speed so high.
She swerves round the last corner
And then throws her sticks high into the blue sky.
Suddenly it's all silent for a moment,
Then everyone cheers.
She is so thrilled with the ending,
She lifts her hands high in the air.

Chloe Wheals (8)
Gaddesden Row JMI School, Hemel Hempstead

Fun!

Most of the time when I have fun,
Is in the holidays, in the sun!
I invite my friends to play,
And we have a splendid day!
They might even sleep round,
We stay up all night and don't make a sound.
That's the time I have fun,
In the holidays, in the sun!

Sîan Worster & Megan Devonald (10)
Kilsby CE Primary School, Kilsby

Don't Shoot

I'm curled up in a corner all on my own,
The rulers are ruling, it's like a king on a throne.
We are the slaves,
No one will misbehave,
Otherwise *bang!*
Everywhere there's banging,
All over the roof bombs are hanging.

The walls are full of children with fear,
You look into their eyes, there's always a tear.
Grown-ups pinned against the wall,
Everyone's crying, even the babies bawl.

Where's my child? I need to go in,
Out of the roof there's flying tin.
I hope my child will survive
Or will she have died?
Oh please, don't shoot, don't shoot.

I want my mum,
Please, Mum, come.
I want my dad,
I'm really sad.
Everywhere there is a single terrorist recruit.
I love you, Mum, I love you, Dad
But please, please, don't shoot.

Sîan Worster (10)
Kilsby CE Primary School, Kilsby

Fire

Fire is hot, dangerous and red
It burns down houses in dread
If you get close you'll drop dead
It's best for you if you have fled.

William Meadowcroft (9)
Kilsby CE Primary School, Kilsby

The Happy Village Of The Dragon

Once upon a crystal-clear morning,
While the sun was still a-dawning,
The dragon gave its fiery warning,
While the people were still yawning.

Time for school, the dragon's rule,
Is that all boys must act cool,
He also says the young girls drool,
I must admit the dragon's a fool.

Time for break at 11.40,
Some of the boys are being naughty,
All the girls are gossiping 'bout laundry,
Some of the teachers are checking out forgery.

Happiness is all around,
Everyone is safe and sound,
They hear the trains in the underground,
There was a teddy lost, now found.

The village of the dragon is lots of fun,
In the boiling, summer sun,
The new school term has just begun,
Lots of homework for everyone.

I forgot to mention, by the way,
Today is the dragon's birthday,
Everyone's singing, hip, hip, hooray,
On this beautiful, sunny day.

The dragon has to go to sleep,
In his dark and gloomy keep,
All the children take a peep,
The dragon snores, they take a leap . . .

Lauren Coates (9)
Kilsby CE Primary School, Kilsby

Beslan

I'm frightened
What's going to happen?
I doubt there's going to be any survivors
I'm hungry
Where's my mum?
I'm too scared to move.

Help!
Why won't they let us go in?
My child is in there
What will happen?
Everywhere silent
Police all around us.

My child!
If I don't get out what will happen?
Where will she go?
There are children screaming
The shooters shooting
I will never get out.

I'm so frightened for them
How could this happen?
I'm the police
What a disaster.

Megan Devonald (10)
Kilsby CE Primary School, Kilsby

Fear

I hear children crying
I hear mini guns firing
Terrorists punching
I hear bombs going off
Blood dripping from the wall
Bodies laying flat.

Charlie Randle (9)
Kilsby CE Primary School, Kilsby

Angry

I get so angry sometimes
Because people pick on me
I wish they wouldn't be mean
They should not call me names
And smash my stuff
Sometimes they push it too far
And I get very angry
And I retaliate.
Angry.

Robert Lloyd (9)
Kilsby CE Primary School, Kilsby

Beslan

They pushed us and hit us with guns
So we went in the gym.
'Go quick or we will shoot you,' they shouted.
We were sat next to the wall.
Someone was crying out loud and got shot.
Bang! The bombs went off.
Bodies were flying across the gym and blood was everywhere.

Robert Burton (10)
Kilsby CE Primary School, Kilsby

My Monster's Face

He has three eyes like a mutant alien.
He has a nose with giant, green rocks in.
He has razor-sharp teeth that can rip through steel.
He has two mouths, his lips are stained red.
He has no ears like a frog.

Haydn Carson (9)
Kilsby CE Primary School, Kilsby

Fun

Sitting under a tree, reading a book
People stare and people look.
The heat is shining on my leg,
Oh look, there is my friend Meg.
We look at my pirate book,
Laughing at Captain Hook.
We are going to the park,
The dogs howl and bark.
We walk back to my house,
The streets are as quiet as a mouse.
I've got to go now,
Goodbye, Meg.

Alice Green (10)
Kilsby CE Primary School, Kilsby

Fun

I shout and laugh and play with my friends,
I always hope it never ends.
My mum calls me in for tea,
And my baby cousin sits on my knee.
Something tells me it's time for a shower,
And my vitamin tablet gets more sour.
I read my cousin a story,
And it gets steadily more gory.
Now it's time for bed,
Goodnight.

Hannah Shuter (9)
Kilsby CE Primary School, Kilsby

Time

Time can move mountains,
Or it can destroy worlds.
It can silence volcanoes,
Or move great icebergs.
Without any time we would not have been born,
But also time can take souls whether we like it or *not!*

Callum Oakley (10)
Kilsby CE Primary School, Kilsby

Trapped

I was so scared, I was shouting, *'Help!'*
I wanted my mum and dad, I was crying too,
The men were threatening me and my friends.
There were bombs hanging from the ceiling.
I was scared.

Jess Wilson (11)
Kilsby CE Primary School, Kilsby

Reptilian Express

Dragon train whistling past
Firing flames and shooting sparks
Teeth in the windows so are the claws
Snakes and lizards at the doors
Picking up Komodo
Picking up the pace
No pretty smiles
No pink lace.

Hannah Ballard (10)
Little Hallingbury CE Primary School, Little Hallingbury

Winter's Peace

As soft as a cloud,
Floating slowly and peacefully,
Drifting down into the fog,
Getting slower
Like it's worn out,
But still drifting,
Into the mysterious atmosphere.
Cautiously walking,
But still not stopping,
Softly spreading all over the land,
Gently rubbing together,
Clouds running away,
Including the fog.
The sun is stretching,
Opening its wings.
All the children,
From many lands,
Are all running around,
Released from their troubles.
Nothing stops their happiness.
It's a lovely winter's day,
It's a peaceful winter's day,
The blanket of calm spreads across the land,
Everyone is now the same,
Our beliefs are all one today,
We are all now children again,
Mothers, fathers, grandfathers, grandmothers,
Even soldiers are today like everyone,
Nations joined by nature's beauty.
We can be as one . . .

Sam De Wilde (10)
Little Hallingbury CE Primary School, Little Hallingbury

Holiday

Holidays are fun, holidays are cool
It's fun to swim and play games in the pool
There's lots of sun and plenty of sand
People make sandcastles that are ever so grand.

There's plenty to do by the sea, people in boats waving at me
Children laughing, running around, lots of fun to be found
My fingers are all wrinkly from swimming in the sea
My feet feel gritty and very sandy.

A long, cool drink is very nice
Followed by a lemon ice
My back is brown, my hair's gone blonde
It's as if someone waved a magic wand.

Crabs creep out from little holes
Children poking them with little poles
Kites flying high along the beach
They're up so far no one can reach.

A girl buries her dad in the sand
His face sticks out and only one hand
People dozing in the cool breeze
Others laughing, each other they tease.

Waves roll in from sea to shore
They never seemed to end, just more, more, more
Birds fly way up high
An interesting place, this big, blue sky.

Relaxed, happy and content is me
And that's what holidays are meant to be.

Sophie Unwin (7)
Little Hallingbury CE Primary School, Little Hallingbury

The Seasons Of A Tree

As spring brings buds to life
And changes their colour to bright green leaves
Then the flowers grow
And the tree changes.

When summer comes
The blossom comes out where the fruit will grow
As blossom falls to the ground and lovely fruit grows
Once grown we pick the trees' beautiful gifts.

Autumn brings the wind
As the tree swiftly sways side to side
The leaves tremble like cradles
Silently and gently dropping to the grass.

In winter the tree sleeps
As still as a statue
As the cold and wet snow gently twinkles down on its branches
Waiting for spring to arrive again.

Aleisha Howes (10)
Little Hallingbury CE Primary School, Little Hallingbury

Autumn

The warm colours of autumn are here
And the bright colours of summer have gone
As the cold days go by winter gets nearer.

Weather is changing from sun to wind and rain
With the hedgehog ready to hibernate again
Birds fly south and other animals make nests.

The colours are warm but the air is cold
All the conkers fall into the palm of cold hands
And farmers harvest and plough the land.

Jack Dann (10)
Little Hallingbury CE Primary School, Little Hallingbury

Untitled

'Time to get up!
Time to get up!'
Mum's shouting upstairs
'Breakfast on the table
Come and get it whilst it's hot.'
Put my football kit on
What a rush
The whistle blows
Everyone goes for the ball.

Running, screaming
It's a free-for-all
What a cheer, 1-0 up
Come on, son, let's get another one!
A pass, a kick, another goal really quick.

2-0 up, what a game
The ref blows his whistle
We won, we won, we won another one!

Taylor Barnett (10)
Little Hallingbury CE Primary School, Little Hallingbury

Personification Of A Tree

The tree starts off as a tiny little seed
And grows and grows
Eventually getting many hands and faces.

The grass, like little people, bows down
As the wind blows
And worships the tree as their god.

The tree stands up on one leg
As it waves to its children, the flowers below
Smiling with many faces.

James Hall (10)
Little Hallingbury CE Primary School, Little Hallingbury

Football Personification

The football match was in full flow
The pitch churned up like a man's face after a boxing match
A dog barking like a child impatient to be subbed into the game.

Trees on the sideline waving like a man
Cheering on the players as they run by
The grass jumping over the bar with the ball like a high-jumper
The net curling round the ball like a mother cuddling her child.

A penalty! The ball flying from the spot like a long-jumper.
A goal! The ball rocketing into the goal like a sprinter.
The boots talking to each other like executives in a boardroom.

The dog finally on the pitch hogging the ball
Like a player forgetting he's part of a team.
The lines smudge under the mud like make-up when a lady cries.
The open goal like the mouth of a cheering man.

Kieran Huggett (10)
Little Hallingbury CE Primary School, Little Hallingbury

Untitled

When you're in class,
Don't play the fool,
Listen and learn,
Then you'll be cool.

Do all your homework,
Don't ever shirk,
If you don't study,
You'll be a berk!

Joseph Jacobs (10)
Little Hallingbury CE Primary School, Little Hallingbury

White Star

White star, there you are
Very high, in the sky.

I look at you, from my bed
Thinking about you, in my head.

You shine so bright,
On this dark night.

Shooting star, moving fast,
Shooting by, shooting past.

When I wake up you won't be there,
That's really not fair.

You will be back again tomorrow night,
That will be a real delight.

Danielle Vaccari Bennett (10)
Little Hallingbury CE Primary School, Little Hallingbury

The Night Mare's Nightmare

The shimmering lights in the sky are back
And so is the big, glowing eye
I can never seem to touch it, even though I try
As I fling my hair out of my face
All I can see is eyes staring back at me, what a peculiar place
Ouch! Stop kicking me, you're digging in my sides
Look at that silly pigeon, I can see him when he hides
I want to be free in the fields and have a good run around
But I have to wander, walking on this hard ground.

Jessica White (10)
Little Hallingbury CE Primary School, Little Hallingbury

What If?

What if the sky was always grey,
Every night and every day,
For ever and ever,
And ever and ever,
I wonder what if?

What if humans were never born,
But the only person was you,
And the rest of the world,
Was run by aliens,
I wonder what if?

What if there was too much food,
But one country didn't get any,
They were starved for food,
But no one helped,
I wonder what if?

What if the world was a happy place,
And no one committed a crime,
But the only horror,
Was you,
I wonder what if?

George Robinson (10)
Little Hallingbury CE Primary School, Little Hallingbury

A Frog's Dream

Frogs are green
And often seen
Jumping up and down a stream.

But how I love my dreams
When they make the girls all scream
Dropping all their green ice cream!

Jonathon Bruce (10)
Little Hallingbury CE Primary School, Little Hallingbury

Fish Tails

Fish, fish, fish,
Make you want to wish
Salmon, trout and tuna - you should buy it sooner.
Good for your brain again and again
Eaten every day, it helps you grow and play.
Eat a bite of shrimp - this will help you think.
Sink your teeth into a crab - you will find it fab.
So healthy, tasty and full of nutrition
Perhaps I will land this
Comp-a-fish-on!

Kirsty Brunton (10)
Little Hallingbury CE Primary School, Little Hallingbury

I Imagine . . .

I imagine swimming through the deep blue sea
and watching all the magnificent colours of the fishes.

I imagine watching the clouds drift over me
and the sun hiding behind them.

I imagine I am flying, seeing things no one has ever seen before.

I imagine I am an animal and I can talk to all of them.

I imagine I live in a chocolate house
with chocolate buttons everywhere.

Emma Shepherd (10)
Little Hallingbury CE Primary School, Little Hallingbury

Lilies

Lilies on ponds, lilies in books,
No wonder they are everywhere because of their looks.
White, pink, purple and red,
Frogs jump and hide, their little feet stick.
Lilies do not last long.

Petals so thick,
They open so wide in the midday sun,
And close when the darkness comes.

Paige Clark (10)
Little Hallingbury CE Primary School, Little Hallingbury

My Dream

In my dream I saw the ball coming towards me
I brought it down and ran with it towards the goal.

In my dream I felt a player foul me inside the box.

In my dream I heard the referee's whistle blow
And he shouted the word, *'Penalty!'*

In my dream I saw myself nervously step up to the penalty spot
And . . .

In my dream I heard the Liverpool fans screaming my name.

In my dream I saw the scoreboard, 10-0 to Liverpool
And my name and ten different times were under it.

In my dream I heard the final whistle of the game
And my best friend on the opposite team, William Holman,
The terrible keeper, came up to me and said, 'Well played.'

Thomas Mitchell (11)
Little Paxton Primary School, St Neots

Untitled

Standing in the
Playground noise
Watching
Young children playing
Boys kicking
Girls chatting
Teachers looking
Whistle blows
Going in
Sitting on the carpet.

Stephanie Smith (8)
Little Paxton Primary School, St Neots

For A Little Friendship

For a little friendship
I would go to the end of the world
I would draw a happy picture
I would make a careful friendship necklace
I would let her live with me
Like the one
Who sits in the garden still.

Jessica Turner (8)
Little Paxton Primary School, St Neots

Who Am I?

My snout is huge and my hair is scraggly,
My gown is blue and my broom is straw,
And my hat is black, pointy and ancient,
My house is haunted, old and gloomy,
Basically I am just a very old lady?

Who am I?

I am a witch!

Laura Baker (10)
Little Paxton Primary School, St Neots

My Nightmare

In my nightmare I saw a devil from Hell Street
He was wearing a brown suit dribbling with blood
He had long, glossy, black hair down to his waist
And eyes that looked like the night sky.

In my nightmare he was sitting on a crooked, black bench
He had his arms folded with a sly look in his eye
He made people feel uncomfortable
He wore a ripped, brown hat over his cheek
To cover his weeping boil.

In my nightmare everything was black and white
All the people were miserable
The only thing that showed colour
Was the Devil!

In my nightmare the Devil was about to attack someone
But I woke up not wanting to know what happened
It was too awful for words.

Chloë Flatman (10)
Little Paxton Primary School, St Neots

My Nightmare

In my nightmare I saw
A bloodthirsty vampire just about to eat me
He had a human's head dripping out of his mouth.

In my nightmare I heard
A tongue licking his lips and blood dribbling.

In my nightmare I saw
Bats flying around myself and a zombie walking scarily around.

In my nightmare I heard
A crackling noise and footsteps . . . *argh . . . !*

Ben Wooldridge (10)
Little Paxton Primary School, St Neots

My Nightmare

In my nightmare I saw
Dark, hidden places
Not meant to be found,
Restricted places like no other.

In my nightmare I heard
Screeching and howling and wind-up noises,
Sounding like chalk on the blackboard.

In my nightmare I saw
Ghosts and monsters glaring at me,
Haunting and circling me.

In my nightmare I saw
A lake like no other,
Filled with blood!

In my nightmare I heard
Shooting and stabbing,
Shouting and screaming.

In my nightmare I saw
My name printed on a gravestone,
As spooky as it sounds,
And as spooky as it looked.

Sam Elias (10)
Little Paxton Primary School, St Neots

What Am I?

I am fast, powerful and a hunter.
I live in the coldest place on Earth
I howl at night at the moon
My white fur keeps me warm.

What am I?

An Arctic wolf.

Tom Humphrey (10)
Little Paxton Primary School, St Neots

My Nightmare

In my nightmare I saw
A deep red pile of flesh covered in blood
That was once a man
In the corner of a derelict house
It was still fresh.

In my nightmare I heard
A blood-curdling scream
Cladding footsteps getting louder and louder.

In my nightmare I thought
I was going to die
I thought I was going to be shot in the head 5 times.

In my nightmare I saw
An axe murderer about to chop my head off
A vampire sucking my blood.

Laurence Cambridge (11)
Little Paxton Primary School, St Neots

In The Park

Sitting on the park bench,
Watching children play.
Playing football in the green field,
Watching children on the big, blue roundabout,
Watching children on the yellow swing.
I want to play football.
I want to play on the blue roundabout.
I want to play on the yellow swing.
I feel upset today because no one will play with me,
With the football team.

Alexander Cronin (8)
Little Paxton Primary School, St Neots

Standing In The Park

Standing in the
noisy park
playing
hide-and-seek
skipping
tag
cat's cradle
Mum calls
time to go
I walk home
happily
quietly
slowly
to my house.

Grace Bell (8)
Little Paxton Primary School, St Neots

Standing In The Playground Noise

Standing in the playground noise
watching
children play
boys racing
girls rowing
little boys
and girls
shouting
whistles blowing
and birds singing
as children
walk in.

Macaulay Clark (8)
Little Paxton Primary School, St Neots

For A Little Friendship

For a little friendship
I would go to the end of the world,
I would carefully draw a light picture,
I would politely build you a house,
I would happily swim the sea,
I would gladly go to the other side of the world,
I would politely share my food with you.
For a little friendship
I would go to the end of the world.

Alyce Mulheron (8)
Little Paxton Primary School, St Neots

Standing In The Riverside Park Noise

Standing in the Riverside Park noise
Watching
Babies crying
Geese honking
Rabbits sniffing
Dogs barking
I walk to the nature reserve
Furiously, sensibly and grumpily
To look at the dinosaur bone.

Tom Wright (8)
Little Paxton Primary School, St Neots

For A Little Friendship

For a little friendship
I would go to the end of the world
I would be a servant if I had to
I would pay your bills for you
I would happily play with you
For a little friendship
I would go to the end of the world.

Ryan Martin (8)
Little Paxton Primary School, St Neots

For A Little Friendship

For a little friendship
I would go to the end of the world
I would give them money if they wanted any
I would buy them clothes and sweets
I would get them a house
I would jump off a bridge
I would even run around the world
For friendship.

Rebecca Minney (8)
Little Paxton Primary School, St Neots

For A Little Friendship

For a little friendship
I would go to the end of the world
I would go to the future
I would travel the world
I would blow up a computer
I would drop a car over a cliff.
For a little friendship
I would go to the end of the world.

Liam Jones (8)
Little Paxton Primary School, St Neots

For A Little Animal

For a little animal
I would go to the end of the world
I would feed it night and day
I would brush and care for it
I would kindly let it sleep in my bed.
For a little animal
I would go to the end of the world
Like the one
Who's calling for me?

Isobel Sewell (8)
Little Paxton Primary School, St Neots

Standing In The Playground Noise

Standing in the playground noise
watching
boys playing catch
girls jumping
teachers walking.
Suddenly the whistle blows
and I walk in slowly
I go in quietly to my seat.

Kirsty Cavanagh-Cole (8)
Little Paxton Primary School, St Neots

For A Little Friendship

For a little friendship
I would drop myself into a volcano
I would fall off a mountain
I would jump off the edge of the world
I would go to war
I would have 24 hours off school.
For a little friendship.

Jacob Hennessy (8)
Little Paxton Primary School, St Neots

For A Little Friendship

For a little friendship
I would go to the end of the world
I would go through a snowstorm
I would make her a friendship bracelet
I would let her live with me
Like the one who sits in the garden
Still.

Deanna Cooper (8)
Little Paxton Primary School, St Neots

For A Little Friendship

For a little friendship
I would go to the end of the world
I would jump off a cliff or live on Mars
I would willingly jump off a building
Or gladly sit on a volcano
I would go to the end of the desert
Just for a little friendship!
I would happily jump down Mount Everest.

Matthew Dawson (8)
Little Paxton Primary School, St Neots

For A Little Friendship

For a little friendship
I would go to the end of the world
I would prepare a loving home
I would lend some money
I would take on holiday
I would celebrate birthdays with presents
I would go to the end of the world
For a little friendship.

Shannon Ferrara (8)
Little Paxton Primary School, St Neots

Fun

Fun reminds me of people playing on the golden sand at the beach,
It sounds like bubbles popping in the air,
It smells like lavender on a giant bush,
It looks like birds flying high in the sky,
It tastes like strawberry jam on toast,
It feels like a rubber band about to ping.

Joshua Dexter (10)
Little Paxton Primary School, St Neots

For A Little Friendship

For a little friendship
I would go to the end of the world
I would stick up for them
I would share my sweets
I would run a mile
I would sleep over
I would play with them
I would buy a present
I would say nice things
I would share my work
I would take them on holiday
I would bake some cakes
I would let them come round
I would swim through a river
I would go to the end of the world
For a little friendship.

Lucy Miller (8)
Little Paxton Primary School, St Neots

Standing In The Playground Noise

Standing in the playground noise
watching
girls rowing
boys fighting
everyone playing
teachers talking
the teacher blows
the whistle
people sad
gently walking
upset
lonely
sat in his place.

Mayson Byatt (8)
Little Paxton Primary School, St Neots

For A Little Friendship

For a little friendship
I would go to the end of the world
I would go through a storm
I would take you on my holiday
I would kindly let you come to my house
I would be willing to let you come to my party
I would make a friendship bracelet
I would go to the end of the world
For a little friendship.

Chloe Futter (8)
Little Paxton Primary School, St Neots

For A Little Friendship

For a little friendship
I would go to the end of the world
I would travel the world just for a monkey
I would travel the globe for anything for you
I would gently and carefully draw you a picture
I would do your work or help you
I would go to the end of the world
For you.

Jemima Hau (8)
Little Paxton Primary School, St Neots

For A Little Friendship

For a little friendship
I would carefully swim a kilometre
I would ski twenty-four-seven
I would parachute off the arch
I would go to the end of the world
I would do anything
Just for some friendship.

Christopher Archer (8)
Little Paxton Primary School, St Neots

For A Little Friendship

For a little friendship
I would go to another world
I would make a friendship bracelet
I would say hello and goodbye
I would go to another world to be kind
I would go to another world to say
'Would you like to go on holiday with me?'
For a little friendship
I would go to another world.

Arabel Collman (8)
Little Paxton Primary School, St Neots

For A Little Friendship

For a little friendship
I would go to the end of the world,
I would merrily share my best comic,
I would climb up sixty huge mountains,
I would eat a spider,
I would jump a thousand times.
For a little friendship
I would go to the end of the world.

Jennifer Bunyan (8)
Little Paxton Primary School, St Neots

For A Little Friendship

For a little friendship
I would go to the end of the world
I would silently sit in the blizzard
I would merrily canoe in the volcano
I would lovingly climb the Empire State Building
I would kindly walk through the space current.
For a little friendship
I would go to the end of the world.

Lewis Dixon (8)
Little Paxton Primary School, St Neots

For A Little Friendship

For a little friendship
I would go the end of the world
I would let them come over for tea
I would kindly take them out
I would kindly take them on holiday.
For a little friendship
I would go to the end of the world.

Charlotte Johnson (8)
Little Paxton Primary School, St Neots

Silence

Silence smells like the musty smell of a forgotten room.
Silence sounds like an eerie crying being echoed across the room.
Silence tastes like a gulp of salty seawater slipping down my throat.
Silence looks like an inky-black night surrounding my face.
Silence feels like the bitter-cold wind lashing against my face.
Silence reminds me of pearly teardrops dripping off a familiar face.

Jessica Lumley (10)
Little Paxton Primary School, St Neots

Kennings Poem

Letter-writer
Phone-ringer
Door-opener
Bell-buzzer
Paper-filer.

What am I?

Timothy Powers (10)
Little Paxton Primary School, St Neots

In My Nightmare

In my nightmare I saw
A fiery dragon devouring a child
Like a brutal, unforgiving beast.

In my nightmare I heard
The morning roar of the Neaman lion
As it slayed its victim.

In my nightmare I saw
Hitler enslaving the world
And the cries of pain as citizens were whipped.

In my nightmare I heard
The roar of battle
As the Spartans were defeated by the Persians.

In my nightmare I saw
A Cyclops destroying a town
Like an immune Titan with burning rage.

Jonathan Miller (10)
Little Paxton Primary School, St Neots

In My Nightmare

In my nightmare I saw
Ghosts floating around the graveyard.
I saw zombies rising from the dead.
I heard the long howl of a werewolf.
I saw slimy, ugly aliens landing on Earth.
I saw a Cyclops gobble up my friends.
I heard screams and shouts coming from all around.

David Cronin (10)
Little Paxton Primary School, St Neots

My Nightmare

In my nightmare I saw
A crook stealing valuable jewels
Shooting at anyone who got in his way.

In my nightmare I heard
A beast roaring
Like it was chasing someone away.

In my nightmare I saw
A zombie touching everyone
And turning them into zombies.

In my nightmare I heard
A gang of beasts
Destroying the village.

In my nightmare I also saw
Aliens transporting me
On their ship.

Kieran Emery & Oliver Cooke (10)
Little Paxton Primary School, St Neots

Fun

Fun reminds me of a playful puppy
Never wanting to stop messing around,
Fun sounds like a lively funfair
With people screaming everywhere you look,
Fun looks like a sparkling sparkler,
Fun smells like a barbecue,
Fun feels like you've just been on a new roller coaster
You have wanted to go on for a long time,
Fun tastes iike something you have not had or tried for ages.

Bethany Fitzgerald (10)
Little Paxton Primary School, St Neots

Laughter

Laughter sounds like people screaming
When they are on a wild roller coaster.
Laughter looks like a balloon floating away into space.
Laughter feels like chocolate melting in your hand.
Laughter tastes like ice cream with all different bursts of flavours.
Laughter smells like sweet strawberries dipped in cream.
Laughter reminds me of bubbles popping in the air.

Sarah Cronin (10)
Little Paxton Primary School, St Neots

My Poem

I have a little furry body
With a stretchy long tail,
Some of us have small ears,
I nibble at my nails,
I run as fast as fast can be
In case a cat is after me.

What am I?

Alex Grogan (10)
Little Paxton Primary School, St Neots

Fun!

Fun reminds me of my Gameboy,
Fun sounds like fireworks blasting in the air,
It looks like popcorn flying up and down,
It smells like bread going mouldy,
It tastes like dark chocolate melting on my tongue,
It feels like jelly on a plate.

Matty Critcher (10)
Little Paxton Primary School, St Neots

In My Dream

Big, sparkling bubbles
And magic, glistening sea
The horizon shining over me.

In my dream I heard
The phoenixes squawking in the sky
And the whistles of the silky dolphin's cry.

In my dream I saw
Unicorns playing and pouncing along
There were trees with bursting bright hearts as big as can be.

In my dream I saw
The hypnotising colours of the sky
The beautiful world that it can be.

I awoke.

Seycha Young (10)
Little Paxton Primary School, St Neots

In My Nightmare

In my nightmare I saw
A great big giant crushing the houses of living people
And the fire going through the people's flesh.

In my nightmare I heard
A growling noise like a tiger
And the screeching noise of the wind.

In my nightmare I saw a man with a sharp sword
Who was about to stab me to death.

In my nightmare I saw a man about to suffocate me
By putting a cushion on my head
Until I was out of breath.

Kieran Dawson (11)
Little Paxton Primary School, St Neots

My Dream

In my dream I saw
A Red Admiral butterfly
Floating on the morning breeze.

In my dream I saw
The birds twittering
High up in the trees.

In my dream I saw
Wild flowers opening in the morning sun
Like a book about to be read.

In my dream I heard
The rushing of a small stream
Like water trickling out of a tap.

In my dream I saw
A deer on the other side of the stream
With antlers branching out like trees' branches
And fur like silk and eyes like marbles.

Daniel Peppler-Jones (10)
Little Paxton Primary School, St Neots

My Nightmare

In my nightmare there are . . .
Spooky skeletons shaking in the dark sky,
Monstrous mummies moaning in a tomb,
Ghostly ghouls grabbing vicious vipers,
Daring devils with three-pronged forks,
Slithering snakes sliding across slimey slugs.
In my nightmare there are
Howling werewolves looking for prey,
Ventriloquists' dummies coming to life,
Dark walls dripping with slime.

Craig Jones (10)
Little Paxton Primary School, St Neots

My Nightmare

In my nightmare I saw
Daring devils dancing around brimstone
Carrying pitchforks as they went.

In my nightmare I saw
Ghoulish ghosts gliding through the midnight air.

In my nightmare I heard
Werewolves howling at the moon
Their eyes as bright as the stars sparkling in the sky.

In my nightmare I heard
Footsteps trampling through the forest
Snapping and crunching branches as they went.

In my nightmare I felt
A zombie touch my shoulder with his cold, dead, bony hand.

Hannah Catalina (10)
Little Paxton Primary School, St Neots

In My Dream

In my dream I saw
Dogs wagging their tails with joy
And children playing with toys.

In my dream I heard
The songs of the ice cream man
And the beiis of the local church.

In my dream I saw
People swimming in the sea
And fish jumping in the river.

Jamie Housden (10)
Little Paxton Primary School, St Neots

On A Bouncing Day

On a bouncing day
I really want to play
On a trampoline
While watching the sun gleam
Bouncing up and down
I was as happy as a clown
But then it made me frown
As the world turned upside down
But as I slipped
I realised I'd back-flipped
I really was amazed
I thought I was crazed
With happiness I was smiling
With joy I was laughing
I heard, 'Well done, well done!
That must be fun.'
And that is the back-flipping story
As I got off with happiness and glory.

Frankie Cuffaro (9)
Lochinver House School, Little Heath

Grommets

First time I had grommets I was just three,
My hearing was poor and I tended to shout,
We went to the doctor's to see what was wrong,
He looked in my ears and said, 'Oh dearie me!'

I went to the hospital to get some first aid
The anaesthetic came with a sharp jab and no more
I went to the theatre with Billy Bonk's
Where Prof Wright worked hard and made it all better.

William Clark (9)
Lochinver House School, Little Heath

My First Trip To Buckingham Palace

High and mighty Majesty,
We visited your high and mighty palace,
The glory flows from the shows,
At your high and mighty palace.
People queue for hours, people wait for days,
To see inside the high and mighty rooms,
Of the high and mighty palace.
Some travel over the sea,
Some by train, bus or walk,
To see Majesty's high and mighty palace.
Long live the Queen!

Adam Kayani (9)
Lochinver House School, Little Heath

I Got In The Football Team

I got in the football team,
I felt as proud as a peacock,
As happy as anything.
I was so relieved,
I was jumping for joy at my first game.

Todd Garber (9)
Lochinver House School, Little Heath

My Bath

Boiling was the water that trickled down my back,
Unpleasant and hot and stinging my skin
Then it became lovely and warm and then cool
The miraculous sound of small rivers running down me
The rivers looked tiny when I had my African bath.

Lorcan Odufuwa-Bolger (9)
Lochinver House School, Little Heath

Moped Mayhem

The streets were whizzing by,
The bike was gathering speed,
We creaked over the hill,
Whoosh! We flew down the mountain,
My brother took control,
The bike screeched to a halt,
The bike came off the ground,
And skidded to a halt.

Zackary Field (10)
Lochinver House School, Little Heath

Desperate To Try

A red board caught my eye,
Desperate to try.
Falling off straight away,
Soon I got the hang of it.
Like speeding over water,
It was *incredible!*

Adam Winston (10)
Lochinver House School, Little Heath

Blue Streak

There was a ripple in the water,
A blue streak moved quickly towards me,
I felt worried for what it might do,
I jumped out the sea as quickly as I could,
Then I saw the bottlenose dolphin looking at me.

Stephen Collis (11)
Lochinver House School, Little Heath

Animal Craft

The ox is in the field,
Like a wrestler in his ring,
Standing strong, tall and proud,
Withstanding every element thrown at him.

The wolf is howling to the moon,
Like a priest praying to God,
Howling, howling, forever howling,
Asking, asking for help.

The panther is in its cage,
Like a prisoner in his cell,
Lounging about in a bored sort of way,
Wondering why he is being stared at.

The chimp is in the trees,
Like a fish in the sea,
Swinging and swimming about,
Having great fun.

Joe Hipkiss (10)
Lochinver House School, Little Heath

The Feeling's Like Flying

Up and away, flying in the sky,
Nervous and very excited,
But nevertheless determined to have a go,
Zooming through the breeze,
Strapped onto rope,
And the feeling's like flying.

Ben Sharer (10)
Lochinver House School, Little Heath

The Jungle

It feels like you are in an oven about to be cooked
All the animals playing about
But you better be careful, a snake may pop out
But the snake will be as colourful as a rainbow.

The jungle will be dangerous
So you better not think it is nicer than a butterfly
You will be sorry you went into the jungle
When the forest is silent you can just hear the animals sleeping
It was worth it.

In the colourful jungle it is as beautiful as a flower
You will see some cute animals
And some that are not nice
You will see monkeys swinging from tree to tree
You will see animals who are as cute as a kitten.

George Green (10)
Lochinver House School, Little Heath

The Nature Mature Maze

Animals cannot escape
Like the sun is in the cloud
And the ant is stuck inside the mud.

The animals are flying away
Like the butterfly is flying in the air
And the plane is on its holiday.

It looks like the animals are resting
The dog is resting in its kennel
Like the car is in its garage.

Harjun Punni (10)
Lochinver House School, Little Heath

The Tide Is Turning
Like Something In A Dream

The tide is turning
Like something in a dream
In the sea
The current takes its hold.

The smooth hound on the seabed
Like a pearl in an oyster,
The newt in the pond
Like a lonely soldier coming.

The garfish in its shoal
Like the water in a millpond
The tide is turning
Like something in a dream.

The ground is dewy
Like a cold winter morning
In the fields
The farmer lets his sheep out.

The cow in his herd
Like the food on the shelves
The oxen in its habitat
Like the stars in the sky.

The ground is dewy
Like the cold, winter morning
In the fields
The farmer lets his sheep out.

Henry Treble (10)
Lochinver House School, Little Heath

The Greatest Place To Be

Chinese everywhere
Not a single face I know
But still I march on.

I was happy and sad
Scared and amused
I was somewhere new.

My thoughts were full
Of questions and more
And all of them were answered.

Alastair Wither (9)
Lochinver House School, Little Heath

The First Time I Was Chosen For A Solo!

Being chosen for a solo,
Pride, joy and excitement bubbled inside me.
Being chosen for a solo,
Made me happy to know that I was good.
Being chosen for a solo,
Made me so nervous I cannot describe.
Being chosen for a solo,
Makes me more alive.

Peter Place (10)
Lochinver House School, Little Heath

Why Was I Nervous?

I went on a stretchy bungee ball
The weather was as hot as an oven
I first felt nervous but then felt great
I hoped I was not going to be dropped.

I saw my family as small as an ant
I felt as tall as Big Ben
On the way back I obviously felt a bit shaken.

Stephen Baldwin (9)
Lochinver House School, Little Heath

Seasons Are Coming

The monkeys are draping on the trees,
Like the coats hanging on their pegs,
The sun is getting darker,
While the animals are going home.

The rabbit is in the field,
Like the soldier is in the war,
The grass is getting riper,
While the herbivores come closer.

The parrot is in the rainforest,
Like colours in a box,
The leaves are crunching up,
While autumn is on its way.

The lizard is frozen on the rock,
Like the banana in its lunch box,
The stem is wafted all over,
While the wind is withdrawing.

The deer is in the wood.
Like negatives in the dark room,
The flowers are opening,
While the clouds go grey.

Arjun Bathia (10)
Lochinver House School, Little Heath

So Soft

She sat there on my hand,
Nibbling her peanut.
She was so soft,
Her fur fluffier than cotton wool.
Her whiskers tickled my hand,
I loved every minute of it.

Jamie Harris (10)
Lochinver House School, Little Heath

Animals (Starring In) Livin' Rough

Humans live in similar places,
But animals are unique,
Humans all live in houses,
But animals are different.

We all live in houses,
But the fish is in the sea,
Like the sugar in the tea,
And the tiger is in the jungle,
Like an apple in an orchard.

We all sleep in beds,
And we all sit in chairs,
But the fox is in its hole,
Like the water in the bottle,
And the bear is in the forest,
Like the money in the safe.

We all do similar things,
Like every bird has wings,
But animals all are different,
Because the otter is in the water,
Like the cloud is in the sky.

Nicolas Edward Alexander Gordon (10)
Lochinver House School, Little Heath

My Grandpa's Stone-Setting

We went into a cold hall
We prayed and it was not small
I felt like crying out loud
Of my grandfather I felt so proud
I stood next to my dad
His strong presence made me glad
I was thinking about grandpa Henry
I hope he was thinking about me.

Mitchell Mayer (9)
Lochinver House School, Little Heath

The Animal Zone

A little newt is swimming
Like a pencil in its case,
Animals running around
In the hills and ponds.

A terrapin under a rock
Like a human in its bed,
Fishes swimming,
Crabs crawling,
An animal's life.

A lizard in a bush
Like a car in its garage,
All animals run around,
But how underground?

A worm in the soil
Like a clam in the sand.
All animals need their freedom.

Alex Savvides (10)
Lochinver House School, Little Heath

Stones Are Not Made For Skimming

Stones are not made for skimming
I tried so hard but Dad was winning.
Dad's was skimming so well
Inside I could feel my heart swell.
My skimming was very bad
My aim was off, just a tad.
Stones are *not* made for skimming
I tried so hard but Dad was winning.
Next time I'd rather go swimming.

Du'aine Davis (10)
Lochinver House School, Little Heath

The Noise At Night

I wake up to a sudden noise,
I run downstairs, outside I fly.
The dog is in his kennel like I should be in bed,
This can't be the noise.

The owl is searching for food,
Like me for the noise,
This can't be the noise.

My dad is tucked up in bed,
Like a rabbit in its hole,
This can't be the noise.

The cat is in the bedroom,
Like the laces on a shoe.
This is the noise!

Oliver Papa (10)
Lochinver House School, Little Heath

My Burger In Georgia

It was a beaming day
My mum had to pay.
It was so tasty
I ate it so hastily.
I loved it so much
It was full of such flavour.
I was so glum when it ended.

It was full of greasy meat
It was lovely when I started to eat.
It was full of crisp lettuce
And I was salivating on my brother.
The ruby sauce would beat all other.

Charlie Avent (9)
Lochinver House School, Little Heath

The First Time I Went To A Golf Tournament

The first time I went to a golf tournament
The weather was wet and windy
But I didn't care
I was at my first golf tournament.

The first time I went to a golf tournament
I was with my friends and family
I was so happy
I was at my first golf tournament.

The first time I went to a golf tournament
I saw plenty of famous people
My brain was buzzing
I was at my first golf tournament.

The first time I went to a golf tournament
I got loads of autographs
My tummy was echoing
I was at my first golf tournament.

The first time I went to a golf tournament
I saw every minute of it
I spoke to Tiger Woods
I was at my first golf tournament.

The first time I went to a golf tournament
I stayed in a caravan
But I didn't care
I was at my first golf tournament.

The first time I went to a golf tournament
I saw all the players
And liked them all
I was at my first golf tournament.

The first time I went to a golf tournament
I wanted anyone to win
I cheered every one
I was at my first golf tournament.

The first time I went to a golf tournament
I loved it all
I just didn't want it to end
I was at my first golf tournament.

The first time I went to a golf tournament
It was an astonishing experience
I had tons of ice cream
I was at my first golf tournament.

The first time I went to a golf tournament
Ben Curtis won
It was amazing
I was at my first golf tournament.

The first time I went to a golf tournament
I got heaps of balls
Now I know what it's like to be at a golf tournament
I was at my first golf tournament.

Sullivan Taylor (9)
Lochinver House School, Little Heath

Noah Returns For The Animals

Noah is approaching
Collecting animals two by two.

First he gets the chickens
While they're fast asleep
They're in their hutch
Like flowers in a vase.

Then he clutches the ants
Hiding in the grass
Like a tiger in the jungle.

Third of all is the zebra
Black and white
It's in its field
Like a sheet of paper full of words.

The dove is last
With its bright, white feathers
It's soaring in the heavens
Like a kite in the sky.

George Lewis (10)
Lochinver House School, Little Heath

The Ball Smacked For A Four

The bowler bowled, speeding really fast
Somebody was out, last bowl caught out
The batsman smacked it for a four
The umpire signalled his hand strangely
I cheered and clapped loud and fast
The bowler was a leg spinner it edged the bat
And the ball was fast spinning in the air
The wicketkeeper missed the diving catch
The ball went over the line for a four
The fielder had a change at last
To be a shining star there was only thirty seconds left
The bowler bowled a really fast bowl
The batsman hit it for a six
The shining fielder leapt up really high
He caught in one hand and he nearly dropped it
The fielding team won by one wicket!

Paras Maroo (9)
Lochinver House School, Little Heath

My First Football Match

When I went to my first football match
I felt really happy and excited.
I was so amazed at how big the stadium was
And also the sight of so many people was brilliant.
When the commentator announced the names of all the players
There were lots of cheers and boos from the crowd.
Just before half-time Fulham scored a beautiful goal
Against Southampton and I cheered and shouted
With all my might.
It was fabulous.

James Hughes (9)
Lochinver House School, Little Heath

Why I Was Doing It Is A Question That Was Never Answered

The look of terror showed on my face,
It was bewildering.
My demise was sure to strike soon,
As I slowly climbed the massive peak.
Why I was doing it is a question that was never answered.
As I felt the thrills, my head was spinning,
I could not speak, I was flabbergasted
As I got off the 150-foot roller coaster.

Jared Bennett (9)
Lochinver House School, Little Heath

Tummies Churning

The atmosphere was buzzing,
With excitement.
The choices of rides,
Amazing.
Tummies churning everywhere.
Voices screaming with fear.
The aromas of fries,
Through our nostrils.

Sailantra Sivathasan (9)
Lochinver House School, Little Heath

Last Week I Went To A Wedding

Last week I went to a wedding
I felt excitement as soon as I got there
What a lovely wedding it was
The bride walked up the aisle
I felt so happy that day.

Luke Clarke (9)
Lochinver House School, Little Heath

The Zone

The Zone is cruel and dark,
The Zone is lukewarm and damp,
The Zone is an excuse for a hellish zoo,
It is a terrible animal camp.

The owl is uneasy; it has been having to hunt
Potatoes instead of mice.
He clings tightly to his fake metal tree branches,
Like a piece of wood in a vice.

He looked out, on guard,
Looking all around the artificial woodland,
His family all killed by disease or humans,
He was the final one to stand.

The Zone, the Zone, the cruel, cruel Zone,
Of tame, noble, great beasts.
Reduced to eating human meals,
Being deceived that they're lucky to have such feasts.

The Astro Turf field of two metres squared,
Is where the African beasts roam.
The lion, having to hunt on this infinitesimal, phoney savannah,
Is dreaming of his home.

He stands like he used to,
Proud and tall, like a soloist on stage.
Then slumps as he remembers the real world -
He is a defeated beast in a cage.

William Thong (10)
Lochinver House School, Little Heath

Cyprus

I was in Cyprus,
Over the blue, blue sea,
I was scared but excited,
Ready to jump with glee.

I could see the fishes,
Beneath my feet,
Ready to join them,
Some time this week!

I was with my dad,
Holding onto him tight,
Knowing it would be bad,
Thinking I would fall into the night.

I was going paragliding,
I was sorry when it had to end,
Hoping to do it again soon,
Sometimes around the bend.

Samuel Fitzell (9)
Lochinver House School, Little Heath

Could It Be?

I walked forward,
Something caught my eye.
Grey, half-buried in the sand between the rocks.
I dug it out,
It was a piece of sharp flint.
I was so disappointed.
I carried on my search.
I looked on the floor and saw a shark tooth!
I was so excited I thought my heart would stop.
Could it be, after my long search, a shark tooth?

Ray Otsuki (10)
Lochinver House School, Little Heath

The First Time I Went To Highbury

The first time
I went to Highbury
I was with my aunty Lynn
All the time I had a grin
Because I knew we were going to win.

The crowd roared
As we scored
They kicked off
And then I coughed.

We got it back
And gave it a whack
And scored!
And the crowd roared.

Then I was naughty
And got a smacked bum.
The final whistle blew.
We won!

Ben Whittington (9)
Lochinver House School, Little Heath

The Sea Was Rough

The sea was rough, the wind was strong
The sand was hot under my feet
I ran down the beach clutching my board
As I plunged into the sea
I jumped, I dived, I swam
Just when a wave as big as a house
Came up behind me
I grabbed my board and I was thrown
Onto the beach on this huge wave
And landed at my dad's feet.

Tom Lewis (10)
Lochinver House School, Little Heath

My First Word

The first time I spoke
The word was 'car'
Something I could see so near and far
Red ones, yellow
Orange and blue
Fast ones, slow ones, big ones too
So remember when you say
The word
James said it too.

Car
Man
Duck
Goose
That's the order till the sentence broke loose.

'Oh golly,' said Mum, feeling very jolly
'He said a word.'
'That's right, Mum and I won't stop now
Because there's more to come.'

Car
Man
Duck
Goose
That's the order till the sentence broke loose.

James Zaremba (10)
Lochinver House School, Little Heath

The First Time I Won A Medal

The first time I had won
Was in two thousand and one,
I was so energetic and filled with fun
I felt like I was shining as much as the sun.

I was in a massive sports hall
Listening to the rules,
Looking at the people swimming in the pools
While my mum and dad were shouting from the stalls.

I was silently sitting down
Feeling like I could wear a crown,
My spirits weren't down.

That was the first time I had won a medal.

Mark Sadler (9)
Lochinver House School, Little Heath

Animals

The monkey is in his playground,
Like a baby in its pen,
The playground full of leaves,
Like the cotton on the baby's leg.

The fox in the forest,
Like a car in the road,
The jungle loaded with trees,
Like the house full of sweets.

The bees making honey,
Like the servant making dinner,
The dog is eating his food,
Like the maid trying the pasta.

Michael Tsiattalou (10)
Lochinver House School, Little Heath

When My Rabbit Got Lost

Feeling sad and scared,
Searching everywhere,
Through the darkness,
Still nowhere to be seen,
Beam of light,
Travelling in the night,
A flash of fur,
A hop in the air,
Back with me,
Safe and sound.

Mattie Glassman (10)
Lochinver House School, Little Heath

A Candle

The golden flame
Is like a person
Running on fire.
The black smoke
Is like black dust
Floating in the air.
The candle wax
Is like a melting ice cream
In the sun.
The candlewick
Is like a burnt match on my birthday
When you light the candles.
The blue part of the flame
Is like a dark blue sky
At night.

Mark Riley (7)
Manland Primary School, Harpenden

Spring

I wake up the golden sun,
Who brightens our misty lives,
I ask him to stretch,
His arms out wide,
He sends his fiery rays,
Down here to brighten all our days,
I like the bright red sun,
With his bright, golden rays,
He floats in the sky,
Like a yellow star,
Because he shines on everyone.

I open up the flowers,
Then dress them in ball gowns,
They dance in the wind,
As I let them spread colour everywhere,
I know they are cheerful every day,
They wave as you pass them,
I let them stand tall and proud,
They smell and look beautiful all day long,
I like them because they dislike no one.

I wake up the animals
From birds to rabbits, even ants and bees,
I see them scamper along the ground,
Happy and cheerful all through the day,
Some fly, some run, they scamper along,
The forest floor,
Through bluebells and snowdrops,
Over logs, under logs,
Round and round all day long,
Some eat nuts and berries,
Some eat other things,
I just really love them all.

Over all of this,
I feel sorry for Sir Winter,
All his ice, frost and snow,
Created the white world,
It glistened everywhere,
He created skiing, snowboarding and ice-skating,
He gave us all Christmas,
Many of which were white,
I really feel sorry for Sir Winter.

I am known as spring,
But then I have to say goodbye!
So summer can come and shine,
Then summer thanks me for preparing
The world for her to use
And turn into summer.

Ellie Duplock (10)
Manland Primary School, Harpenden

Tornado

He destroys by kicking,
Then sucks it all up.
Houses flying,
Children crying,
People dying,
In daytime or in night,
He doesn't care,
Destroying is just an ordinary dare.
Every living thing
Scatters to move out of his way.
He concentrates on his next one.
It could be the next day?

James Elliott (10)
Manland Primary School, Harpenden

Wolf

In the daytime I'm gentle and kind,
But as darkness approaches, you will find,
That I am dangerous, fierce and cruel,
You should be cautious to not get covered
By my slimy drool.

I sneak and steal, howl and bite,
I give little children a terrible fright,
I hide in dark alleys, whilst on the prowl,
With a sniff, a scratch and a ferocious growl.

I should think by now that you can tell,
That I turn into a creature from Hell,
By the name of wolf I scavenge the street,
Searching and searching for morsels to eat.

James Harding (11)
Manland Primary School, Harpenden

The Candle

The candle is like
A flickering fairy light
On a Christmas tree
On a snowy Christmas morning.
It's like a slice of butter
Melting on your knife.
It's like a volcano erupting
In the sunrise.
It dazzles like the disco balls
At the midnight feast
And disco.

Amy Robinson (7)
Manland Primary School, Harpenden

Winter

I sweep across the country
Covering everything that I see
With my great, thick, white blanket
Making everything look like Antarctica
I shower everyone with my tiny little pearls.

I tear all the leaves off all of autumn's branches
I watch all the children making snowmen all day long
I invite Mr Santa Claus to give presents to everyone
I chase flocks of birds to a warm place in the sun
I blow cold air to make the lakes turn to crystal.

I make hats and scarves to keep everybody warm
As I blast through the trees I break off wood for firewood
I sometimes laugh too loudly and conjure up a storm
That makes people frightened and they all go indoors.

I give them all hot chocolate and a fat, delicious turkey
They all light their Christmas trees
And then stuff themselves with turkey
They open all their presents
I hear shrieks of joy
They all go to bed joyful and exhausted.

I am *winter.*

Angus McKay (10)
Manland Primary School, Harpenden

The Sun

The sun shot out of bed and flew to the sky,
He smiled cheerfully about making all the people happy,
He circled the universe finding the interests of the world,
Shining over Australia, Japan, Europe and much more,
Getting tired in his breathless race trying to catch the moon,
He eventually made his way back home
And fell asleep after an exhausting day of hard work.

Tom James (10)
Manland Primary School, Harpenden

The Sun

I'm the sun, I'm ever so hot,
I glow and shine and sizzle a lot.
My heat is such I burn in earnest,
For I'm a fierce and fiery furnace.

Sometimes I'm kind and sometimes I'm not,
The people on Earth think I look like a spot.
But that's a mistake, and for that they'll pay,
'What's happened to the sun?' they'll say.

Behind the clouds I shall stay all day,
For everyone wants me to go away!
Their skin is so fair, they get very burnt,
To hide away is what I have learnt.

But what I like best is to shine out so bright,
And this is the way I give out lots of light!
So go out in the sun while I am still there
For soon I will set and the sky will be bare.

Duncan Merelie (10)
Manland Primary School, Harpenden

Toucy, Toucy!

I am a toucan bird.
I flap my wings rapidly.
Whatever you have heard
I don't do things placidly.

I am not very pleasant.
I always push and shove
And I am in my element
When I'm in the sky above.

Jack Fenton (10)
Manland Primary School, Harpenden

The Sun

In the darkness of space sits the sun
Always like a sleeping nun,
Although he may be a blazing general
But all his friends just call him yellow.
With his care plants can grow
Even we should know!
The blinding light in the sky
Is the sun strolling by.
With his strength he lets us live,
And without him we would die.

Christopher Martin (10)
Manland Primary School, Harpenden

Hurricane

The hurricane's fast arms are about to destroy,
His legs are in the land of Troy,
While children and adults are sobbing in pain,
'Ha, ha!' shouts the hurricane.

His evil, flaming, deadly eyes,
Look up to torment the threatening skies,
All of a sudden clouds start crying,
And the hurricane starts dying.

Oliver Jackson (10)
Manland Primary School, Harpenden

The Sun

Come on, clouds, I'm in a hurry!
Get out of my way.
Let the people look at my beautiful face.
I am the largest, brightest, most powerful star in the sky.
I work so hard to make you all happy.
Growing your food and wrapping you in warmth
And yet you forget I am here at all.

Richard Murray (10)
Manland Primary School, Harpenden

Sunlight

Gleaming through the open window,
Casting shadows on the wall,
Shining like a glow-worm.

Passing through the bright, blue sky,
Showering my rays upon the sea,
Deep orange, shimmering yellow, ruby-red,
Light the day ahead.

I turn the sky from dismal grey to vibrant blue,
I am daytime,
I am summer,
I am life,
I am the *sun.*

Katie Moore (10)
Manland Primary School, Harpenden

The Moon

I am a kind and glittering light
Shining through out the night.

I travel from the far east to the far west
Trying to do my utmost best.

I let my silver, dazzling hair fall around me
It spreads like butter all over a lone tree.

I have travelled around the world
And at night I have let my light come unfurled.

I feel happy with all my stars out and bright
And I think I'm important because I'm the brightest thing at night.

Oliver New (10)
Manland Primary School, Harpenden

The Dark One

I am the shadow,
The velvet blanket,
I am the one who hides in corners,
Turning slowly away from the sun,
I am the unknown,
The dark one.
I am the one who creates night,
Putting out all light,
I am the thief,
The ruler of the night.

I sometimes sneak up your garden,
Stealing trees and smothering houses,
At Hallowe'en and in winter,
Christmas too,
I open up and drown you in shadows.
I am hidden,
For I am darkness.

Francis Priestland (10)
Manland Primary School, Harpenden

The Sun

The dazzling sun smiles as she looked down.
She tiptoed past the moon trying not to wake him.
The sun is proud to see all the people
Smiling and being joyful.
She chuckled in delight.
She was happy.
She started dancing.
'Oh, I am so glad to be me!' she cried.
Can you say the same?

Charis Parker (11)
Manland Primary School, Harpenden

Water

There she standeth with all her divine beauty,
But beyond her face, beyond her innocent, beautiful face,
Hidden in her stunning eyes there is a terrible secret,
Which only ye wise old wind can see.

But inside her resplendent, shimmering shell,
She is evil, deathly evil,
But let us be silent as she tells her treacherous tale.
'O woe is me, the wind has slain my husband,
He wreaked his vengeance on my love,
He says I deserve it,
He says I'm a wolf in a sheep's skin,
But I'm not, really, I'm not,
Please come and ride the waves with me,
And I'll take you to the depths beyond.'
An evil smile played on her lips.

But alas her victim escaped.
'You fool, you can't escape me, I'm water.'
But the victim did not come back.
Suddenly her eyes turned blood-red,
And a great wave arose from the water,
Like horses stampeding.
The great wave washed over her,
And the forest around the clear stream was peaceful again.

Naomi Reeve (10)
Manland Primary School, Harpenden

My Name Is Ivy

I creep around the garden,
I venture up the wall,
And if I'm in the mood,
I go next door to call.

I worm my way through brickwork,
That's rough and dry and coarse,
With my rapid growing,
And my brutal force.

I spy on all the humans,
Of course I know them all,
I know their personalities,
And everyone how tall.

I've outgrown all the trellis,
And everything in sight,
There's nothing now to climb upon,
That uses all my might.

My worst fear is commencing,
I'm dying, can't you see,
A human is now coming,
To chop the life from me.

Edwin Reynolds (10)
Manland Primary School, Harpenden

Grey Wolf

The grey wolf proud of his slick, grey coat
He prowls unseen, unheard like a scout
Moving with stealth.
Stalking his prey, hungry for dinner
A baby racoon dies too soon
The wolf bored now, lopes off.

George O'Connor (10)
Manland Primary School, Harpenden

The Boastful Fox

I sneak around
And spy
I live in a den
With my family
I master every move
As I am the best.

I almost slither
And then shout, *'Boo!'*
It is a cosy den
With the best family
I definitely am the best
As everyone else is rubbish.

I am the supreme fox!

James Riley (10)
Manland Primary School, Harpenden

The Candle

The candle flame flickers
Like rays of the sun going down below the horizon.
Its wax trickles down the edges
Like a leaking bottle about to burst.
It's as warm as a sizzling barbecue on a summer's day.
It springs like an animal about to attack its prey on a late evening.
Its wax is as sticky as a lump of glue, almost dry.
It sways gently like someone on a swing slowly rocking.
It's as burning as a hot, enjoyable sausage.
The flame is as bright as the moon shimmering away on a
moonlit night.

Holly Sach (7)
Manland Primary School, Harpenden

The Victorious Vine

I am crawled on which I hate,
Bugs think I'm second-rate.
I live right next to a human home,
But I wish I could roam.
I'm so very strong,
And a poisonous green,
Plus I'm brilliantly long.

When you think you're having a conversation privately,
You're not,
Someone can see,
And that someone is me.

I hold captive a tree,
He can't escape from me.
I have slithered around him,
I will squeeze him until he dies.
Him I'll never unwind,
Because I'm a victorious vine.

Aran Tattar (10)
Manland Primary School, Harpenden

The Sun!

So bored with travelling around the world every 24 hours.
The sun sighed and groaned and the clouds came out.
She used to dance about cheerfully lighting up the sky
But now, always so tired, the sky only cries.

The sky turns to bright as the sun glares through.
The clouds get out of her way.
Then thunder joins the sun in her misery.

Milly Walpole (10)
Manland Primary School, Harpenden

The Candle

The candle flame sounds like
A fire burning sticks into ash
Never to stop until the sunrise.
The candle flame looks like
A dragon with a blinding burst of fire
When it's really angry.
The candle flame looks like
A dart racing through the sky
Like in a dart championship.
The candle flame looks like
A machine gun bullet
Ferociously firing during a battle.
The candle flame dazzles like
The sunrise coming up from the horizon.
The candle flame looks like
A bomb almost ready to explode.
The wax falling from the candle looks like
The sweat slipping down a man just finishing a marathon.
The candle flame looks like
The flame on a barbecue.

Joshua Sambrook (7)
Manland Primary School, Harpenden

The Candle

The candle flame burns like
An exploding volcano.
The wax falls in blobs like
Snow on Christmas Day.
The wax burns like
White chocolate on a birthday cake.
It makes beautiful light
To light up the room.
It shines on the world like
The scorching sun.

Isabelle Smith (8)
Manland Primary School, Harpenden

The Plane

Only
a
huge,
amazing,
big,
large,
spacious,
immense,
gigantic,
powerful
aircraft can glide like an eagle
fly like a bird, and make as much noise as
a packed football stadium. It holds lots of
people, holds
lots of
luggage.
It's good
in an
aeroplane
because
you're going
on . . . *holiday!*

Liam Walker (10)
Manland Primary School, Harpenden

The Rainbow Waterfall

As I sit and see the waterfall looking at me,
Rushing past, crashing rocks.
What a sight to see!
As I sit and stare,
The more I start to see the rainbow
In the waterfall reflecting on flowers bigger than me!

Charlotte Morley (9)
Manland Primary School, Harpenden

The Candle

The candle leaps into life like
A spitting gold tongue.

The candle flame is like
A dragon breathing fire.

The candle flame is like
A warm and hot burning fire.

The candle flame is like
A red diamond shining on a necklace.

The candle is as quiet
As a sly thief on a dark, silent night.

The candle flame is like
A hot burning sun in the hot desert.

The smoke is like
A cloud which is going to burst out with rain.

Joanna Asquith (7)
Manland Primary School, Harpenden

The Candle

The orange flame leaping like
A tiger trying to get its prey.

A candle is like
A dragon blowing out its fire from its mouth.

The candle leaps like
A dolphin jumping in the water.

The candle smoke is like
A rain cloud on a thundery day.

The candle is like
A hot, dazzling smoke.

Brynmor Willis (7)
Manland Primary School, Harpenden

A Candle

The smoke of the candle is like
A little choo-choo train in the distance.

When the wax is melting it's like
A hill with snow and children going down it.

The flame is like
An orange surfboard in the sea with someone on it.

Shadows slip across the wall like
A thief in black clothes.

Hannah Sweeney (7)
Manland Primary School, Harpenden

A Candle

The flame is like
A poppy waving in the countryside,
It is like
A boxer's glove in the middle of battle.
It is like
A scorching sun beaming down on the Sahara Desert.
The wax falls like
Snow pouring down a mountain.

Matthew Wright (7)
Manland Primary School, Harpenden

The Candle

The candle flame jumps like a big dolphin.
It shimmers like orange crystal.
The orange flame flickers into life, it swishes this way and that.
The flame is like a Chinese dragon with its hot, hot, boiling fire.
It gallops like a hot, hot horse.
It's like a dancing ballerina twirling and twirling.

Emma Dobson (8)
Manland Primary School, Harpenden

The Candle

The candle flame burns
Like a fire
Just been set alight.

The candle flame gleams
Like a powerful torch
While the wax slowly melts.

The candle flame bobs up and down
It lights the way through the night
Like the street lamps.

The candle flame burns
Like the fiery sun,
It is as sparkly as the sea.

The flame of a candle is very special to people at happy times
And sad moments too
But cheer up because it's Christmas!

Hayley Everett (7)
Manland Primary School, Harpenden

The Candle

The flame is like
A pouncing tiger in a dangerous forest.

The fire is like
A leaping ballet dancer on stage.

The glowing flame is like
A star on a bright night.

The flame is like
A roaring lion's mane.

The sparks are like
Popping fireworks on Guy Fawkes' night.

Lorna Sullivan (8)
Manland Primary School, Harpenden

The Candle

The orange candle flame flickers up and down
Like a tigger when it jumps.

It shines in your face
As if you are getting blinded by a torch.

It is like the sunrise.
It blinds you so you can't see.

The candle smells like a bonfire
And you choke after it.

It's like when somebody's making a barbecue
In the evening.

The candle flame flickers like a raindrop
Racing down the window.

It melts like an ice cream.

Melanie Garrihy (8)
Manland Primary School, Harpenden

The Candle

The candle flame is like a rabbit
Springing up and down,
Like a fox hunting the rabbit.
The smoke of a candle is like a spirit
Rising from its grave.
The flame is like a shot from a tank
In the Great War.
It shines like a diamond
In total darkness.
The candle flame sparkles
Like ten suns.

Luke Holroyd (7)
Manland Primary School, Harpenden

The Candle

The flame is like a shot of volcano in Hawaii
On a hot, boiling day.

The candle's colour is like shimmering gold
In a hot, sizzling witch's pot.

The candle wax is like a chunk of white chocolate on the fire
On a cold winter's day.

Joey Jackson (8)
Manland Primary School, Harpenden

The Candle

The candle springs to life
It flickers like a volcano exploding.
It's like the trees dancing in the wind
On a hot summer's day.
It burns like the sun at midday.
It wiggles like a snake dancing.
It's like the shooting stars orbiting the Earth.

Harry McKay (7)
Manland Primary School, Harpenden

The Candle

Candle, candle comes up like me
Getting up in the morning.
Hot like a dragon's breath.

The wax is like melting white chocolate
On a hot, summer's day.
The flame dives like a champion swimmer.

Edward Kennington (7)
Manland Primary School, Harpenden

Best Friends

We have some secrets, just us four,
My friend, her friend and some more.
We always meet up all together
And probably will forever and ever.
We always giggle and giggle some more,
It's great fun, just us four.
We have sleepovers and go out for lunch too.
We do lots of shopping sometimes until we're black and blue.
We always giggle and giggle some more.
It's great fun, just us four!
We like to make up dances and have cheese straws for snacks.
We like to read magazines and love to sit down and relax.
We always giggle and giggle some more.
It's great fun, just us four.
So as you can see, my best friends to me
Are really special and great fun to me.
We always giggle and giggle some more.
It's great fun, just us four!

Louise Asquith (10)
Manland Primary School, Harpenden

The Candle

The orange flame flickers like the golden sun on a bright morning.
Then it shines as bright as a light in the night.
It glows like a star.
It smells like a pumpkin on Hallowe'en.
It shoots like a firework in the night.
It shoots and twirls like a rocket in space.
It shivers like an aeroplane getting ready to go.

Eleanor Morley (7)
Manland Primary School, Harpenden

Water

Water is everywhere
In the bath
In the shower
Drip, drip
Drop, drop
Down the drain
Down the hole
Drop, drop
Drip, drip
Down it goes
Down the river
Slosh
Sloosh
Splosh
Splosh
Through
The pipe
In the shower
Onto you
Ripple, ripple
Down your nose
Cross your eyes
And look, look
At it
Rippling
Down your
Face
Look at it
Dripping and dropping
And sloshing
And slooshing
And plopping
Down and
Drip, drip.

Abigail Browning (9)
Manland Primary School, Harpenden

My Parents Are Aliens!

My parents are aliens
because when they tell me to tidy my room
I bet they are communicating to other aliens
as to when to destroy the planet.
My parents are aliens
because when they send me to school
they go back to their home planet Mars
and tell everyone to come and visit Earth.
My parents are aliens
because when they send me to bed
I hear gadgets being built to have a conversation with Mars!
My parents are aliens
because in the morning when they get changed
they close the door.
I bet it's because they have green lizard skin!
My parents are aliens
because when they have a conversation
as soon as they see me they quickly change it.
My parents are aliens
and I bet yours are too!

Hania Corbett (10)
Manland Primary School, Harpenden

Flowers

Flowers are red with raindrops on.
We have yellow ones, pink ones in different sizes.
There are white ones with yellow middles,
Blue ones with a butterfly sitting on a green leaf.
Green leaves poking out of tulips and daffodils
Or maybe buttercups.
The beautiful little yellow ones
Or even maybe velvety, red roses.
So don't pick the flowers,
They are there to grow to make the world a happy place.

Emily Douglas (9)
Manland Primary School, Harpenden

Magical Gardens

Flowers come up every year
The colours on them look so clear
Red ones, yellow ones, purple or blue
There's loads of colours to choose from
It's all up to you
Gold, silver or even pink
There are so many to choose from
Just look and think.
Butterflies are colourful little things
They've got lovely patterned wings
Some are patterned striped
Some are patterned spot
But it doesn't matter which ones
Because it's the whole lot
Butterflies fly around
But never ever make a sound.

Claudia Harris (9)
Manland Primary School, Harpenden

Bubbles

Bubbles are like rainbows
Bright in the sky
Beautiful as a bumblebee
Swimming in the air
Travelling in the sky
Building up to make giant bubbles.

Diving in the sky
Like dolphins
Dashing in the air, so fun.

So free as I feel myself going
Pop! Pop! Pop!

Joanna Illingworth (9)
Manland Primary School, Harpenden

People

People, people everywhere, seeing a lot of them at the fair.
Walking round and round all the stalls, trying to win a prize.
Suddenly the sky goes dark, everyone runs to where they parked.
Before the heavens pour down with rain.
Oh goodness me, here comes the sunshine again.

Sophie Armstrong (10)
Manland Primary School, Harpenden

A Candle

The orange flame is a glowing, bright star in the evening sky.
The candle flame jumps like a dragon's hot fire from its mouth.
The wax of the candle drips like a blanket of white silver snow.
The flame jumps like a blue dolphin the dark, deep, blue sea.

Oliver Pollard (7)
Manland Primary School, Harpenden

Water

Water is ice-cold as it drops onto my skin.
Water is super soft like cotton wool when it's on the ground.
Water we all like and we like it because it does lots of things for us.

Megan Howey (9)
Manland Primary School, Harpenden

Hate

Hate is like black, stormy clouds
It sounds like a bat
It smells like a snake
It reminds me of shouting
It looks like lightning
It feels like a motor.

Jason Hamilton (7)
Peartree Primary School, Welwyn Garden City

Happiness

Happiness is green like grapes
It tastes like fresh kiwi
It looks like butterflies
It feels like stars
It smells like chocolate
It sounds like music
It reminds me of all my family.

Kayleigh Plunkett (7)
Peartree Primary School, Welwyn Garden City

Love

Love is red like strawberries
It looks like a book
It tastes like strawberries
It feels like a fluffy cloud
It smells like home
It sounds like music
It reminds me of the computer.

Liam Burt (7)
Peartree Primary School, Welwyn Garden City

Love

Love is pink like getting married.
It reminds me of flowers.
It smells like perfume.
It looks like hearts.
It feels like fluffy clouds.
It sounds like birds singing.

Danielle Skutela (7)
Peartree Primary School, Welwyn Garden City

Happiness

Yellow is like the sunshine
It sounds like birds singing
It smells like calm perfume
It reminds me of presents
It feels good inside
It looks like a thousand pounds.

Leandar Mugadza (7)
Peartree Primary School, Welwyn Garden City

Fear

It tastes like rotten oranges
It looks like all mouldy goo
It sounds like a ghost
It reminds me of scary movies
It feels like a wet day
It smells like salt.

Novuyo (Millie) Ntaisi (7)
Peartree Primary School, Welwyn Garden City

Sadness

Sadness is like a red petal falling off a flower
It feels like someone hurting me
It reminds me of someone kicking me
It looks like soft cotton wool
It smells like onions.

Emily Hawkins (7)
Peartree Primary School, Welwyn Garden City

Fear

Fear is like a ghost
It looks like a sheet
It tastes like cotton wool
It feels like plastic
It smells like salt
It sounds like wind
It reminds me of a dark night.

Jordan Saba (7)
Peartree Primary School, Welwyn Garden City

Happiness

Happiness is pink like a pink pig.
It tastes like strawberry milkshake.
It smells like chocolate.
It looks like fluffy candyfloss.
It feels like melting marshmallows.
It reminds me of beautiful flowers.

Amanda Bakewell (7)
Peartree Primary School, Welwyn Garden City

Anger

Anger is red like a bee sting
It tastes like blood
It feels like cold, hard metal
It looks like a violent person
It sounds like someone screaming
It reminds me of a buzzing wasp.

Aidan Carter (7)
Peartree Primary School, Welwyn Garden City

Love

Love is like a red rose.
It smells like perfume.
It sounds like butterflies flying past.
It tastes like pink ice cream.
It feels like getting married and you have good inside you.
It reminds me of birds singing.
It looks like a thousand pounds.

Chantel Mawdsley (8)
Peartree Primary School, Welwyn Garden City

Sadness

Sadness is blue like rain
It tastes like rotten apples
It sounds like heavy rain
It feels like a heavy heart
It looks like grey clouds
It smells like fish
It reminds me of a lump in my throat.

Chloe Martin (7)
Peartree Primary School, Welwyn Garden City

Happiness

Happiness is blue like the salty sea
It tastes like cheese and onion crisps
It smells like a swimming pool
It looks like the sun
It feels like you have got a new toy
It reminds me of going on a long trip with my friends.

Tanvir Ahmed (7)
Peartree Primary School, Welwyn Garden City

Love

Love is red like strawberries
It feels like a soft pillow
It smells like lemons
It reminds me of playing on the PS2.

Keegan Manley (7)
Peartree Primary School, Welwyn Garden City

My Dog

I have a dog called Guinness,
He is a bit of a menace,
His fur is silky,
His teeth are milky.

His nose is wet,
He hates going to the vets,
He has got soft, velvet ears,
He hates people crying tears.

He is two,
He goes crazy when the cows go moo,
He loves his friends,
When they start playing their fun never ends.

I love my dog!

Madeleine Murchie (8)
Preston Primary School, Hitchin

Tiger

Down in the deep, dark, Bengal forest,
If you look really hard,
You will find a tiger.

But this is no ordinary tiger.

Down in the deep, dark, Bengal forest,
If you find this tiger - you must shout out:

Tiger mama-papa!
Tiger mama-papa!
Tiger mama-papaaaaaa!

Down in the deep, dark Bengal forest,
There is one thing you have got to do -

Run!

Alexandra Higgin (9)
Preston Primary School, Hitchin

Panda

I have a panda that's black and white,
Who eats morning, day and night.

After breakfast it will climb the tree,
And will stay there all day till it's time for tea.

When night-time falls he will curl up small and dream of me.
When he wakes up there is me waiting with his cup of tea.

He has a friend called Pandchi,
Who likes to join panda for his morning tea.

Then they eat and eat till both are full,
When night falls they say, 'Night-night.'

Gemma Hutchinson (8)
Preston Primary School, Hitchin

Creation

The sun made the plants to dance and prance.
The trees were told to be tall.
The air made the sea be all wavy.
The clouds told the sky to be bright blue.
The grass was dyed green by the daisies.
The ducks and swans were put in the pond
And told to swim gracefully.
Our friends and family were told to be loving, kind and caring
And make us laugh.
The bushes were told to put blackberries on themselves
And told to be eaten by the birds.
Everyone was told to laugh and have fun
Under the big, yellow sun.

Tyla Garrett (10)
Preston Primary School, Hitchin

Candy My Guinea Pig

Small and round,
Soft and brown,
He eats all day and charges all around,
I pick him up and brush him down.

A treat he eats on my lap,
While my mummy cleans out his place to nap.

Clean straw and hay,
He chews all day,
I love my guinea pig,
More each day.

Georgina Chalk (7)
Preston Primary School, Hitchin

The Teacher's Day In Bed

The teacher has the flu
So she sent her pets to school . . .
There's a monkey to play the piano
A gorilla to teach games
An octopus to teach art
A snake to teach reading
A seal to bring them in
An elephant to water the plants
A hippo to teach dancing
A cheetah to teach gym
A panther to teach hymns
A turtle to teach running.

Scott Porch (7)
St Brendan's Catholic Junior School, Corby

The Teacher's Day In Bed

Our teacher is very ill.
She sent her pets to school instead . . .
There's a parrot to teach the class on the board
An owl to do the reading
An adder to teach the art
A monkey to watch the class
A tarantula to give the books out
A giraffe for dinner duty
A cheetah to teach games
A tortoise to stop cars
And a zebra to get the children.

Ross Gormley (7)
St Brendan's Catholic Junior School, Corby

The Teacher's Not At School

The teacher is not at school
So she sent her pets instead . . .
There's a penguin to read the register
A pig to sharpen pencils
A lion to teach handstands
A monkey to give out bananas
A crocodile to teach singing
An elephant to do snack time
A dolphin to teach swimming
A seal to do PE
A gorilla to teach climbing trees
A parrot to teach maths
A zebra to help them across the road.

Brogan Ennis (7)
St Brendan's Catholic Junior School, Corby

The Teacher Is Not At School

Our teacher is having a day in bed.
She sent her pets to school instead . . .
There's a parrot to do the reading,
A hummingbird to teach singing,
A gorilla to look out for trouble,
A jellyfish to start the computer,
An alien to clean the room,
A fish to teach us to swim,
A monkey to teach games,
A crocodile to teach reading,
A zebra to get children across the road.

Charlie Nunn (7)
St Brendan's Catholic Junior School, Corby

The Teacher's Day In Bed

Our teacher is in bed ill.
She sent her pets instead . . .
A parrot to do the register
A wolf to sharpen pencils
A robin to teach singing
A monkey to do games
A dog to do the school dinners
A lion to do a quiz
An owl to do reading
A hummingbird to do drama
A gorilla to do gym
A zebra to do the plays.

Sam Mahon (7)
St Brendan's Catholic Junior School, Corby

The Teacher's Day In Bed

Our teacher is very ill.
She sent her pets instead . . .
There's an octopus to play the piano
A seal to water the plants
A dolphin to give swimming lessons
A lion to teach eating
A monkey to do games
An ostrich to teach reading
A bear to teach handwriting
A kangaroo for art
An adder for maths.

Sonny Doherty (7)
St Brendan's Catholic Junior School, Corby

The Teacher's Day In Bed

Our teacher is having a day in bed.
She sent her pets to school instead . . .
On the way to school the octopus carried 8 animals.
There was a parrot to teach the children to read
An elephant was sweeping the leaves on the playground
The giraffe was on playtime duty
An octopus was doing maths and sums
The zebra was helping the children to cross the road
The dolphin helps the children to swim.

Sinead Hyldon (7)
St Brendan's Catholic Junior School, Corby

The Door

(Based on 'The Door' by Miroslav Holub)

Go and open the door
Maybe there's a comedian in the front garden
Maybe there's a clown dancing in the moonlight
Maybe there's a chatting cat talking to someone
Maybe there's a satellite spying on us in the night.
Go and open the door.

Conor Hoare
St Brendan's Catholic Junior School, Corby

The Teacher's Day In Bed

Our teacher's having a day in bed.
She sent her pets to school . . .
An octopus to water the plants
An elephant to play games
A butterfly to watch the children
A cat to teach dancing.

Molly Crainie (7)
St Brendan's Catholic Junior School, Corby

Jungle

In the jungle there are lots of animals,
Some big, some small
But all nice and tall.

In the jungle there are lots of animals,
Monkeys, tigers
And lots more.

In the jungle there are lots of animals
That love to play
All night and day.

Ruth Lydia Johnson (7)
St Brendan's Catholic Junior School, Corby

All About Autumn

Autumn has come, summer went.
We are going to miss the flowery scent.
Leaves are green all about
And some are red without a doubt.
I feel sorry for young and old
Who have to live in the freezing cold.
We are going to miss the hot sunshine
That we had in the beautiful summer.

Jenna Gormley (8)
St Brendan's Catholic Junior School, Corby

The Door

(Based on 'The Door' by Miroslav Holub)

Go and open the door
Maybe there's some aliens invading the street
Maybe there's a man waiting by the bus stop
Maybe there's a monster running everywhere
Maybe there's an ogre in the green slime.
Go and open the door.

Jack Scales (8)
St Brendan's Catholic Junior School, Corby

The Door

(Based on 'The Door' by Miroslav Holub)

Go and open the door
Maybe there's a hot-air balloon that's popped
And landed on our house
Maybe there's a hippo making waterfalls
Maybe there's a croc drinking water
Maybe there's a croc chasing his tail
Maybe there's a giraffe nodding his head.
Go and open the door.

Jack Connolly (8)
St Brendan's Catholic Junior School, Corby

Elephant

Elephants are really big.
Lions are really fierce.
Eagles are really fast flyers.
Parrots are really good speakers.
Hippopotami are good swimmers.
Ants are good at climbing trees.
Newts are good hiders.
Tigers are fast runners.

Harriet Sumnall (7)
St Brendan's Catholic Junior School, Corby

The Door

(Based on 'The Door' by Miroslav Holub)

Go and open the door
And there might be a flying knight
Maybe there's a gingerbread man who's lost his head
Maybe there's a chair with lot of hairs on it
Maybe there's a man who's got a tan.
Go and open the door.

Hannah Mahon
St Brendan's Catholic Junior School, Corby

The Door

(Based on 'The Door' by Miroslav Holub)

Go and open the door
Maybe outside there's a horrid triceratops munching our grass
Maybe there's a theatre with all the stars dancing and singing
Maybe there's a castle with horses in a stable
And black knights guarding the gates
Maybe there's stars swirling around the moon
With their flashing lights.
Go and open the door.

Connor McShane
St Brendan's Catholic Junior School, Corby

The Door

(Based on 'The Door' by Miroslav Holub)

Go and open the door
Maybe there's an alien dancing the night away
Maybe there's a tree kissing a lamp post's feet
Maybe there's a lamp post praying to a tree
Maybe there's a giant destroying the town
Maybe there's a giant dog licking all the buildings.
Go and open the door.

Sean Horne (8)
St Brendan's Catholic Junior School, Corby

The Door

(Based on 'The Door' by Miroslav Holub)

Go and open the door
Maybe outside there's a pancake eating a human
Maybe there's cats and dogs falling from the sky
Maybe there's a giant worm attacking the city
Maybe there's a monster smelling his toes.
Go and open the door.

Jack Carson (8)
St Brendan's Catholic Junior School, Corby

The Crazy Food Poem

I eat my ice cream with cheese,
I've done it all my life,
I always fall on my knees,
My mum tells me to cut it with a knife.

My monkey drinks his tea with butter,
He thinks it is very funny,
When he has it he starts to mutter,
He does so much talking
No wonder he has so much money.

Ryan Campbell (9)
St Brendan's Catholic Junior School, Corby

My Name

My name is Fionnuala
I don't really like my name
People call me 'Nula'
But I'm always the best at games.

What I like to eat

I like soup and gravy
With a slice of bread
My brother wants to join the Navy
While I go to bed.

Fionnuala McGrory (9)
St Brendan's Catholic Junior School, Corby

Peculiar Foods

I eat strawberries with gravy,
It's always been that way,
It takes a certain bravery,
But I eat it every day.

Chloe Collins (9)
St Brendan's Catholic Junior School, Corby

The Door

(Based on 'The Door' by Miroslav Holub)

Go and open the door
maybe outside there's another world
with grass so green and flowers,
it's such a lovely sight.

Maybe there's a little tree
that bends down to smell the flowers below him
that smell so pretty.

Maybe there's a forest with trees
that sway in the breeze
with lots of little butterflies that try to talk to me.

Maybe there's a little city
with busy traffic and even a little pond.

Go and open the door.

Annabeth Ure (8)
St Brendan's Catholic Junior School, Corby

The Door

(Based on 'The Door' by Miroslav Holub)

Go and open the door
Maybe there's a cow doing The Cha-Cha Slide on a car
Maybe there's a roadrunner sitting drinking beer
Maybe there's a lamp post swimming in the lake
Maybe there's a monster running across the world
Through the sea and land.
Go and open the door.

Eleanor Conway (8)
St Brendan's Catholic Junior School, Corby

The Door

(Based on 'The Door' by Miroslav Holub)

Go and open the door
Maybe outside there's a chicken doing the moonwalk
Maybe there's a train talking to itself
Maybe there's a dog reading a joke book
Maybe there's a boulder made out of ice cream.
Go and open the door.

Danielle Dempsie (9)
St Brendan's Catholic Junior School, Corby

The Door

(Based on 'The Door' by Miroslav Holub)

Go and open the door
Maybe there's a gushing river flooding the whole of the street
Maybe there's an octopus weeding the flowers
Maybe there's an angel floating down from Heaven
Maybe there's a haunted house standing in the street.
Go and open the door.

Beth Davidson (8)
St Brendan's Catholic Junior School, Corby

The Door

(Based on 'The Door' by Miroslav Holub)

Go and open the door
Maybe there's clouds that have turned to candyfloss
Maybe there's a big group of pigs flying in the sky
Maybe there's a giant doughnut in the centre of the city
Maybe the characters from all the books have come alive.
Go and open the door.

Luke Connachie (9)
St Brendan's Catholic Junior School, Corby

The Teacher's Day In Bed

Our teacher is having a day in bed.
She sent her pets to school instead . . .
A kangaroo to do PE
A monkey to teach English
A dog to go on duty
A bush baby to serve the children's meals
An octopus to teach art
An owl to read them stories
A stingray to teach the children to work the computer
A parrot to announce the assembly
A dolphin to teach them how to swim
A chimp to teach the children drama
A zebra to help the children cross the road.

Nina Conway (7)
St Brendan's Catholic Junior School, Corby

The Door

(Based on 'The Door' by Miroslav Holub)

Go and open the door
Maybe outside there's a baby bird hatched from its yellow egg
Maybe there's an ocean with golden surroundings
Maybe there's a brand new world with flowers so sweet
Maybe there's a dazzling white castle with roses on the door.
Go and open the door.

Emily McClymont
St Brendan's Catholic Junior School, Corby

Cat Food And Dog Food

My dog eats cat food and dog food
He's done it since he was born
He acts like he is such a dude
It always makes him yawn.

Darcey Nolan (9)
St Brendan's Catholic Junior School, Corby

The Door

(Based on 'The Door' by Miroslav Holub)

Go and open the door
Maybe outside there's a knight in shining armour
On his handsome horse
Maybe there's a dragon, hot and ruby-red
Maybe there's a cave, dark and glum and wet
Maybe there's a hole that can make you go to China.
Go and open the door.

Chloé McLaughlin (9)
St Brendan's Catholic Junior School, Corby

The Door

(Based on 'The Door' by Miroslav Holub)

Go and open the door
Maybe there's an ocean made of purple potion
Maybe there's a donkey racing down the street
Maybe there's a takeaway sitting on the doorstep
Maybe there's a whole new world waiting to be explored.
Go and open the door.

Francis Kelly (8)
St Brendan's Catholic Junior School, Corby

The Door

(Based on 'The Door' by Miroslav Holub)

Go and open the door
Maybe outside there's a fish walking along the vast street
Maybe there's a dog climbing up a tree
Maybe there's a forest with no trees in it
Maybe there's a cat walking on the clouds.
Go and open the door.

Joseph Smyth (8)
St Brendan's Catholic Junior School, Corby

The Teacher's Day In Bed

Our teacher is ill in bed.
She sent her pets instead . . .
There's a bush baby to teach art,
A cobra to teach drama,
A manatee to teach swimming,
A turtle to watch people at playtime,
A hedgehog to teach games,
An adder to teach maths,
An echidna to teach spelling,
A humpback whale to listen to reading,
An electric eel to work the computers,
A zebra to get children across the road.

Harry Garvey (7)
St Brendan's Catholic Junior School, Corby

Families

Families are really kind
And they take care of you.
Me and some of my family go everywhere together.
In my house I have a loving family.
Long ago when I was a baby I used to get lots of help.
You know my family, they love me.
Sometimes they go mad at me but I know they still love me.

Caoimhé Friel (8)
St Brendan's Catholic Junior School, Corby

Marmite And Toast

My dog eats Marmite and toast
My brother thinks it's mad
It's what my dog likes most
It eats it with my dad.

Corey McGovern (9)
St Brendan's Catholic Junior School, Corby

Try This!

I like chocolate and Marmite
It's always been that way
It gives my sister such a fright
And makes her run away!

I like cream and dog food
I started when I was three
Mum thinks I'm just being rude
But it's a real treat!

Shay Doherty (9)
St Brendan's Catholic Junior School, Corby

Weird

I eat crocodile soup with cream
I've done it since I was four
It makes my sister have a bad dream
But I'll always ask for more.

My friend eats spaghetti with jelly
I know that it sounds weird
It rumbles in his belly
Then it makes him grow a beard.

Connor Keenan (9)
St Brendan's Catholic Junior School, Corby

The Door

(Based on 'The Door' by Miroslav Holub)

Go and open the door
Maybe outside there is a pig drowning in a swamp
Maybe there's a hippo climbing up my house
Maybe there's a chicken climbing up a lamp post
Maybe there is a waterfall made of coca-cola.
Go and open the door.

Honor Reilly (8)
St Brendan's Catholic Junior School, Corby

Cornflakes With Honey

Cornflakes with honey
I eat cornflakes with honey
My mum said I'm mad
It is kind of funny
I am kind of glad.

Slimy wobble
My friends eat worms in jelly
They've done it since they were five
I heard it in their belly
It sounded like bees in a hive.

Sean Porch (9)
St Brendan's Catholic Junior School, Corby

The Door

(Based on 'The Door' by Miroslav Holub)

Go and open the door
Maybe outside there are man-eating pigs.
Maybe there's the man on the moon sitting on the sun.
Maybe there's a chimney growing in the sky.
Maybe there's chickens doing the conga on the road.
Go and open the door.

Roisin Reilly (8)
St Brendan's Catholic Junior School, Corby

Weird

I drink coffee with veg
I've done it since I was three
It's got a strange edge
But I prefer it more than tea!

Aiden Hamill (9)
St Brendan's Catholic Junior School, Corby

The Teacher's Day In Bed

Our teacher is having a day in bed.
She sent her pets to school instead . . .
There's a seagull to do the register
And a tiger to sharpen pencils
A bluebird to teach the singing
And a squirrel to teach the reading
An elephant to water the plants
A monkey to teach the piano
And there's a goat to hoover the room
A giraffe to watch the children at playtime
An octopus to teach the games
And a zebra to help the children to cross the road.

Louise Docherty (7)
St Brendan's Catholic Junior School, Corby

The Teacher's Day In Bed

Our teacher's not at school.
She's staying in bed because she broke her leg
So she sent her pets instead.
Mrs Mind has 4 pets
A roadrunner to teach running
A parrot to teach singing
A bird to teach maths
A seal to teach swimming.

Beckie Manning (7)
St Brendan's Catholic Junior School, Corby

Crisps And Custard

I eat crisps with custard
It's always been that way
Sometimes I lick mustard
And dream about it night and day.

Conor O'Donnell (9)
St Brendan's Catholic Junior School, Corby

The Teacher's Day In Bed

Our teacher is very ill.
She sent her pets to school instead . . .
A gorilla to teach a quiz
An elephant to water the plants
A monkey to teach games
An octopus teaching at the computers
A parrot to teach singing
A crocodile to do the reading
A shark to give swimming lessons
An owl to teach the children to fly
A giraffe to teach art
A rhino to teach drama
A jellyfish to do piano lessons
A canary to do handwriting
A zebra to get the children across the road.

Sophie Theobald (7)
St Brendan's Catholic Junior School, Corby

In Spring

In spring animals are born,
Baby ducks, baby cows, on a lovely day,
Everyone likes spring with hay and corn,
Children are playing in a good way.

Flowers grow a lot in spring,
The plants grow and grow and grow,
Trees have leaves where the birds are flying,
New ducks are swimming, watch them flow.

Spring is a good time,
When animals are made,
Lots of new monkeys climb,
The sun will never fade.

Shaun Kingston (8)
St Brendan's Catholic Junior School, Corby

All Different Animals

A nimals are lovely and soft
L adybirds are spotty and small
L ions are like the king of the jungle

D ogs are wild and also pets
I love animals especially horses
F oxes are greedy and also sneaky
F lamingos are pink and stand on one leg
E lephants are huge and loud as well
R abbits are cute and cuddly
E agles swoop down to catch their prey
N ests are to keep birds' eggs safe
T igers are fierce and love to sleep

A nts are tiny and black
N ew animals come in spring
I nsects fly around in the sky
M oths stay still all through the day
A pples are juicy and caterpillars eat them
L izards change colour
S nakes slither around and are scary to some people.

Michaela Higgins (8)
St Brendan's Catholic Junior School, Corby

The Teacher's Day In Bed

Our teacher is having a day in bed.
She sent her pets to school instead . . .
There's a squirrel teaching about acorns
An owl teaches how to read
A dolphin to teach them how to learn to do a backflip
A penguin to teach how to dive into the water
But the penguin was scared of the water
A monkey teaching how to swing
A zebra was making sure that they were crossing the road safely.

Sally O'Keeffe (7)
St Brendan's Catholic Junior School, Corby

The Teacher's Day In Bed

Our teacher is very poorly.
She sent her pets to school instead . . .
There's a parrot to read poems
An octopus to play the piano
A dragon to cook the food
A rabbit to teach dancing
A canary to teach flying
A robin to teach singing
A dolphin to swim and dive
A crocodile to brush teeth
An electric eel to make the computer work
An elephant to hoover
A pig to clean the table
A tiger to look out everywhere
A zebra to get children across the road.

Rachel Mackie (7)
St Brendan's Catholic Junior School, Corby

The Teacher's Not At School

Our teacher has got the flu.
She sent her pets to school instead . . .
There's a shark to teach games
An elephant to water the plants
A lamb to teach handwriting
A dog to teach art
An owl for teaching drama
A lion to teach reading
A monkey to make sure everything is right
A cheetah to teach the piano.

Feyi Lawal (7)
St Brendan's Catholic Junior School, Corby

A Teacher's Day In Bed

Our teacher has the flu today.
She sent her pets to school instead . . .
A monkey to read the register
A lion to sharpen pencils
A pigeon to teach singing
A goat to hoover the room
An owl to teach history
A dog to teach games
An ape to help play piano
An elephant to water the plants
And a zebra to get the children across the road.

Ilanah Tromans (8)
St Brendan's Catholic Junior School, Corby

The Teacher's Day In Bed

Our teacher is having a day in bed.
She sent her pets to school instead . . .
There's a monkey to do games
A shark to sharpen pencils
An owl to do the register
A hummingbird to teach singing
An octopus to play the piano
An elephant to mark the work
A giraffe to teach tricks.

Kieran Murray (7)
St Brendan's Catholic Junior School, Corby

Silly Food

I eat my pizza with mustard,
I eat it every day,
I think it tastes like custard,
In a funny sort of way!

Jordan Carey (9)
St Brendan's Catholic Junior School, Corby

The Teacher's Day In Bed

The teacher is ill.
She sent her pets to school instead . . .
There's a gorilla to teach games
A chipmunk to teach children to sleep with their eyes open
A snake to do the quiz
A coyote to do playtime duty
A jellyfish to teach swimming
A monkey to teach drama
A zebra to get the children across the road.

Thomas Doherty (7)
St Brendan's Catholic Junior School, Corby

The Teacher Is Not At School

A crocodile does multiplication to children
A parrot likes to read
A monkey plays on the swing
A giraffe looks out for people having fits
An octopus reads the register
A pig cleans up the tables
A gorilla plays peek-a-boo
A hippopotamus teaches swimming lessons
A zebra to get the children across the road

Alice Clements (7)
St Brendan's Catholic Junior School, Corby

The Crazy Dessert Poem

I eat my custard with my jam
I've done it since I was born
I do it with my brother Sam
We eat it on the lawn.

James Barrowman (9)
St Brendan's Catholic Junior School, Corby

Soy Sauce

Soy sauce
I eat my spaghetti with soy sauce,
It's always been that way,
It makes me feel like a horse,
And it makes my friends stay away.

Honey
I eat my sausage with honey,
It's always been that way,
It makes the skin go sunny,
And that is what I say.

John-William Hughes (9)
St Brendan's Catholic Junior School, Corby

Fab Food

I eat ice cream with carrots,
It's always been that way.
I gave it to my parrot,
And then it flew away.

I eat jelly with custard,
I've done it since I was five.
I had a bit of mustard,
And I felt alive.

Melissa Swinton (9)
St Brendan's Catholic Junior School, Corby

Strawberries With Gravy

I eat my strawberries with gravy,
I know it may sound mad,
My mum thinks that I'm crazy,
Because I share them with my dad.

Liam Fahy (10)
St Brendan's Catholic Junior School, Corby

My Poem

I eat my sausage with butter,
It's always been that way,
It makes my belly flutter,
Then I fly away.

I eat my beans with curry,
I've done it since I was born,
I think I'm in a hurry,
Then I blow my horn.

I eat my chocolate with rice,
I've done it since I was five,
It tastes very nice,
It makes me really alive.

Ryan James Meredith (9)
St Brendan's Catholic Junior School, Corby

Strange Food

I eat my carrots with honey,
It's always been that way,
It moves in my tummy,
And I eat it every day.

My dog drinks custard,
He drinks it every day,
My mum puts in a little mustard,
And then she runs away.

Chelsea Brown (9)
St Brendan's Catholic Junior School, Corby

Delicious Food From Me

My goldfish likes his ice cream hot
He eats it every day
I think he eats it in a pot
His birthday is in May.

Lisa Shaw (9)
St Brendan's Catholic Junior School, Corby

My Poem

I eat my fish with curry,
I've done it all my life,
I like to eat it in a hurry,
But I even use a knife.

I eat my beans with curry,
It's been that way ever since I was born,
I like to be a hurry,
In case my mum beeps the horn.

I eat my sausage with butter,
It's always been that way,
I like to mutter,
But that is in the day.

Louie David Munro (9)
St Brendan's Catholic Junior School, Corby

Bizarre Meals

I eat my mash with thyme,
I've done it since I was six,
It tastes nothing like lime,
Or even like a Twix.

I eat my sweetcorn with cream,
It's happened since I was born,
When Mum sees it she turns green,
And runs away forlorn.

I drink my tea with gravy,
It's always been like that,
My brother calls me crazy,
I just use his winning bat.

Rhowanna Cable (9)
St Brendan's Catholic Junior School, Corby

Never Together Food

For breakfast my dog eats jam and salmon,
It's always been that way,
But for dinner it has a bit of gammon,
He eats it almost every day.

I drink my tea with a slosh of mustard,
I've done it all my life,
Then I wash the taste away with custard,
Normally I drink it with a knife.

Lauren Bradshaw (9)
St Brendan's Catholic Junior School, Corby

My Poem

I eat my custard with jam,
I've done it all my life,
I think it tastes like ham,
It gets me in a lot of strife.

I drink my milkshake with gravy,
I've done since I was five,
I know it must sound crazy,
But it certainly keeps me alive.

Ryan Colbert (9)
St Brendan's Catholic Junior School, Corby

Unusual Food

I eat my custard with gravy
I've eaten it since I was five
It tastes all hot and runny
It keeps me happy and alive.

Iain Smith (9)
St Brendan's Catholic Junior School, Corby

Family Meals

My dog eats cheesecake and gravy,
It's always been that way,
It drives the cat crazy,
It stinks of it every day.

My cat eats cream and jam,
It's always been that way,
He has a topping of ham,
This is what his favourite is every day.

I drink hot chocolate with peas,
It's always been that way,
I wash it down with tea,
I always make Dad pay.

I eat jelly and custard,
It's always been that way,
I don't like it with mustard,
I have it anyway.

Steffan Baillie (9)
St Brendan's Catholic Junior School, Corby

Silly Poems

My rabbit drinks hot chocolate and gravy
It's always been that way
It has a lot of bravery
I wouldn't do it anyway.

I eat peanuts and jelly
It's always been that way
Wibble, wobble goes my belly
I do it every day.

Louis Mutch (9)
St Brendan's Catholic Junior School, Corby

The Funniest Thing You Have Ever Tasted

I eat my cake with custard,
I've done it all my life,
And then I wash it down with mustard,
And I cut my cake with a knife.

I eat my sandwich with gravy,
I've done it since I was five,
I got it from a lady
But it still keeps me alive.

I eat my peas with ice cream,
I've done it all my life,
But it makes my mum scream,
And I don't use a knife.

My goldfish eats human food,
He's done it all his life,
But the vet said he should,
And he does it with a knife.

Allan Getty (9)
St Brendan's Catholic Junior School, Corby

The Life Of Food

I drink my tea with fish
I've had it all my life
And eat it in a dish
And pick it on a knife.

My cat eats sugar with ham
It's always been that way
Then it tries to kiss this man
Now he hides in hay.

My pig has curry with pie
And loves it every day
Then tells a little lie
Then runs away.

Selorm Lazare (10)
St Brendan's Catholic Junior School, Corby

The Award Ceremony

Building bat boxes,
Placed high in the trees.
Small animal boxes for mice, voles and shrews
But we never got to go to the award ceremony.

Cleaning out the pond,
Found frogs, newts and shrimps,
Water snakes zigzagging through the water
But we never got to go to the award ceremony.

Digging up turf for the flower garden,
Wheelbarrow whizzing around,
Planning and planting, how it's done
But we never got to go to the award ceremony.

Cutting down trees, pruning back plants,
Chopping back the weeds,
Clearing the paths
But we never got to go the award ceremony.

Moving the logs,
Snapping off branches and twigs from the trees,
Put in a pile and hoped for animals to make a home there
But we never got to go to the award ceremony.

Marcus Hill & Jake Stride (8)
Stapleford School, Stapleford

The Art Attack

Sploshy, splashy, it goes everywhere
All different colours going here and there.
Paintbrushes going everywhere
Ending up flying in the air.
When they fall back down, they go splat!
Squelching under people's feet, messy as they walk,
They get on with their work and we just talk, talk, talk!

Lily Doyle (7)
Stapleford School, Stapleford

Playground

I wanted to play Lucy's game
She said, 'No!'
I cried, I begged
She said, 'No!'
I asked Olivia if I could borrow her action adventure rope
She said, 'No!'
I asked, I pleaded
She said, 'No!'
I then asked Phoebe and Holly if I could play their game.
They said, 'Yes!'
I smiled, I laughed and played with them.
Olivia and Lucy saw our game.
They came over and begged and pleaded
And we said, 'Yes!' and were friends again.

Chanelle Tollervey (8)
Stapleford School, Stapleford

Playtime

When I go to play I like chase games,
Playing with my friends,
Making funny names,
Chasing round the field.
Sometimes we like to be silly,
Playing on the climbing frame,
Swinging upside down,
Getting very dizzy.
Playing with the grass,
Tossing it around,
Getting very itchy.
I love playtimes.

Imogen Mead (7)
Stapleford School, Stapleford

School Rules

Don't swap any of your gel pens,
Don't give any of your snack.
Always put your toys away,
Unless you want a smack.

Don't fight in the classroom,
Leave it till home instead.
Always put your work away,
It could cost you your head.

Never run on tarmac,
Be careful not to touch people on the bars.
Quickly, the head teacher is coming,
So let's play cards.

Feed the fish at lunchtime,
Don't fiddle with anything in class.
Never start a food fight,
Don't ever smash the glass.

Always be kind to animals,
Never stomp on the floor.
Always be kind to the teachers,
Don't ever slam shut the door.

Never be nasty to your friends,
Don't get in a mood.
Always clear up your mess,
Don't just gulp down your food.

Chanelle Tollervey (8)
Stapleford School, Stapleford

Pirates

A pirate came this morning,
Brandishing a sword.
He put me in a dirty sack
And shouted as he warned:

'Don't you move a muscle,
You dirty little imp.
I'm taking you hostage,
If you move you'll sink.'

He took me to his dirty ship,
He tipped me from the sack.
He said, 'Get to work, you dirty dog,
Make sure you don't slack.'

So I got to work,
And scrubbed the deck.
I made it shine like gems,
Then suddenly there was a crash, the ship turned to a wreck.

Bang! Bang! went the cannons.
Clash! Clash! went the swords.
I jumped off the edge.
'Man overboard!'

The salty sea splashed my face,
But I could swim quite well.
And then the tide swept me to shore,
And everything was swell.

Amy Thomas (10)
Stapleford School, Stapleford

Animals

A is for antelope, jumping around
B is for badger, safe and sound
C is for cats, cuddly as can be
D is for dog, playful you see
E is for elephant, stomping about
F is for frog, they jump I've no doubt
G is for giraffe, their necks are so long
H is for horse, they're big and strong
I is for iguana, they're creepy little things
J is for jay, have you heard them sing?
K is for kangaroo, they jump around a lot
L is for leopards, they have lots of spots
M is for monkey, they swing from the trees
N is for newt, they swim in the reeds
O is for octopus, of legs they have eight
P is for parrot, it says, 'Alright, mate!'
Q is for queen bee, she thinks she's the best
R is for robin, they have a red breast
S is for snake, slithering as they go
T is for tortoise, they are so slow
U is for unicorn, they have a sharp horn
V is for vulture, they fly about at dawn
W is for whale, as big as can be
X is for X-ray fish, they live in the sea
Y is for yak, with big, fluffy hair
Z is for zebra, they have stripes everywhere.

Molly Sidebottom (9)
Stapleford School, Stapleford

God

If God were a colour
I think it would be
White as a swan,
As pure as me.

If God had a taste
I think it would be
Sweet like a cookie,
Like I have with my tea.

If God had a smell
I think it would be
Fresh as fresh like perfume,
Or salty like the sea.

If I knew what God looked like
I think it would be,
As pure, as clean
As you would like Him to be.

Now you know what I think God looks like,
We can talk about His name,
And about what it means.

G is for great.
O is for old.
D is for delicious.

Tian Howell (9)
Stapleford School, Stapleford

Chronology

I had my first step when I was a baby,
I ate a bug, maybe, maybe.
When I was a baby I bounced in my bed,
But I broke Panda's teddy, I ripped off the head.
When I was four I learnt to tie my lace,
But when I was three I tipped cake over my face.
Now I'm eight, I've got a new bike, all wonderful and red,
I pedalled to the fair, I won a blue ted.
I'm nowhere near nine but Tipey is getting fat,
She's had four babies, they were born on the mat.
I want to be a star, a cook or a vet,
If I do I'd be looking after hundreds of pets.
I'll plan to have a family, one girl, one boy,
When they're eight I'm going to buy them loads of toys.
When I'm adult I'll cook loads of food,
I'll be a cool chef, I'll be a cool dude!

Phoebe Tucker (8)
Stapleford School, Stapleford

Rainbow

Red is for valentine where love goes,
Orange is for drinking, I pour and it flows,
Yellow is for sun as it shines,
Green is for grass as it grows,
Blue is for the sky like in the game I Spy,
Indigo is my bedroom where I like to lie,
Violet is my favourite, I like this one the best.

Each time I see a rainbow,
It makes me feel glee,
As every single colour has
A special meaning to me.

Beth-Anne Tyler (9)
Stapleford School, Stapleford

My Friend And Me

My friend and me will always be
Like a bumblebee and a flower
My friend and me will be together forever, ever and ever and ever
That's my friend and me.

My friend and me will play together forever
My friend and me will dance around the tree
My friend and me will shout out to the sky,
'We are friends forever.'
That's my friend and me.

My friend and me don't look the same
But we both have friendship
My friend and me will fill our years with glee
Even when we go our different ways.
That's my friend and me.

Rebecca Bryant (10)
Stapleford School, Stapleford

Animals!

A is for ant crawling on the ground.
N is for newt so slimy and icky.
I is for iguana, I don't want one of those.
M is for monkey that has gone mad.
A is for antelope that is very annoying.
L is for lion that roars in my ear.
S is for snake that hisses in the night.

Abby Brown (10)
Stapleford School, Stapleford

Dance And Ballet

Dance

D is for dancing, let's have some fun
A is for Anastasia bumping the beat
N is for nervous, doing a dance
C is for crazy, I feel the heat
E is for energy, we have lots of it.

Ballet

B is for ballet, what else can it be?
A is for astonishing ballet I always do
L is for how I like to do a big show
L is for how I like to do a dance
E is for the earrings I put in my ears for the show
T is for the tutu, frilly and pink.

I am sorry to say this is the end
Of the ballet and dance link!

Georgia Fiddes (9)
Stapleford School, Stapleford

Football Crazy

(Inspired by 'The Sound Collector' by Roger McGough)

The new coach came to the football,
Dressed in tracksuit red and grey,
Put every sound into a bag,
And carried them away.

The screaming of the people,
The whacking of the ball,
It's flying through the air,
It missed the goal and smacked against the wall.

The coach came to the football match,
And didn't leave his name,
Unless he comes back some day,
Football will never be the same.

Harry Pateman (10)
Stapleford School, Stapleford

Dance!

I'm only best at dancing
Nothing else you see
I like to dance to pop and jazz
And also R'n'B!

I also like to tap dance
But break dancing isn't me
My friends all say that I am brill
I like to dance with glee!

Ballet is the hardest
Positions 1, 2 and 3
To be a perfect dancer
You have to dance like me!

My favourite dance is modern
I'm best at that probably
I like to dance and jump about
And make myself go crazy!

Elly Dewen (10)
Stapleford School, Stapleford

Poetry

Sitting down at my desk, thinking what to write,
So many things in my head, finding hard to pick.
Raging fires, fearsome wolves or maybe a scented forest.
Loud things, quiet things.
Lot of ideas but just one to choose.
Oh, just which type to have?

Olivia Mannall (7)
Stapleford School, Stapleford

Games, Glorious Games

Games, glorious games,
What couldn't we wish for?
Right, all along the Thames,
Kids playing what they wished for,
TV, equals a ball,
Oh, games, wonderful games,
Marvellous games, glorious games.

PS is at the top,
So that's why we like it a lot now,
We made 'Ratchet and Clank',
Bolts, weapons, we thank,
Oh, games, wonderful games,
Marvellous games, glorious games.

Xbox they say is 'naff',
But I think it's good enough now,
'Halo' the game of the bests,
Lazers, jets and cadets,
Oh games, wonderful games,
Marvellous games, glorious games.

Nintendo, the oldest here,
My dad always drinks beer watching,
So Mario pops,
And glows as he goes.
Oh, games, wonderful games,
Marvellous games, glorious games.

Harry Crawford (10)
Stapleford School, Stapleford

The Once Upon A Time Rhyme!

Once upon a time there was a funny rhyme
of royalness and sweetness, of wickedness and crime.

It starts with Cinderella, a sweet girl when she came,
she had two evil sisters, boy, that was a shame.

Then we have Snow White, she likes to clean the house,
her friends are very strange, a mongoose and a mouse.

Of course there is Rapunzel, with her long, thick hair,
oh God that wicked witch, she wasn't very fair.

Then there's Sleeping Beauty, sleeping was her game,
of course she was famous - then she had the fame.

We go on to the evil, I am really starting to shake,
I'm getting very frightened, this is a big mistake.

We have the wicked Hook, he fought Peter Pan,
he had an evil sidekick who drank from a can.

Cinderella's stepmother is skinny and a bore,
she never does the cleaning, she's demanding more and more.

The evil fairy had a wheel, which had Sleeping Beauty asleep,
the handsome prince came to save her, which awoke her
dreaming sleep.

We've finished the poem of prettiness and crime,
we have to have a happy ending to finish off this rhyme.

Rebecca Walker (9)
Stapleford School, Stapleford

Sound Collector

(Inspired by 'The Sound Collector' by Roger McGough)

The new coach came to football
Dressed all in blue and grey
Put every sound into his car
And carried them away

The cheering of the fans
The flapping of the chairs
The chatting of the commentators
The rushing up the stairs

The diving of the keeper
The kicking of the ball
The turning of the programme
The whispering by the kids from school

The gulping of the drinks
The scoring for the team
The flushing of the toilets
The training for the football scheme

The moaning of the referee
The shouting of the fans
The blow of the whistle
The creaking of the stands

The running of the players
The booing for Man U
The rushing of the taps
The singing by you

The new coach came to football
He didn't leave his name
Left us all in silence
Football will never be the same.

Elliot Barling (9)
Stapleford School, Stapleford

Horse Riding!

H is for horses grazing in the field
O is for obstacles for the horses to jump
R is for riding for abilities to build
S is for saddle to avoid all the bumps
E is for exercise, keeping them warm

R is for rhythm, make sure it's right
I is for in the stables where foals are born
D is for dressage, the steps are light
I is for injury, oh how it hurts
N is for noise, the cheer of the crowd
G is for gallop, you'll never see me.

Now you know about riding,
How 'bout you try it?
Much safer than gliding,
Come on, I'm not lying!

Lois Hutchings (10)
Stapleford School, Stapleford

Football Sounds

F is for the fans, the noisy lot.
O is for *oof!* A player just got hurt.
O is for *ooo!* We just missed a goal.
T is for typical, we lost 2-0.
B is for boys, no girls can play.
A is for all of us dressed in black and red
L is for lots of fans, nearly 9001.
L is for luck, that's all we have left.

S is for soon, soon it is over.
O is for Owen, he's just got substituted.
U is for unfair, we got a yellow card.
N is for nothing, nothing has gone wrong.
D is for *do it!* We can do it harder!
S is for superb! We just won 5-2!

Alex Sandell (9)
Stapleford School, Stapleford

My Music!

Music I do love the best
Including R'n'B
Now everyone thinks I am mad
They don't wish they were me!

Pop I like the best
Next comes R'n'B
I really like to jump and shout
I think it's really me!

My music makes a real good noise
But only cos it's loud
Soon I will get earache
But still I'm very proud!

Music I do love the best
Including R'n'B
Everyone may think I'm mad
But certainly not me!

Hannah Juniper (10)
Stapleford School, Stapleford

Winter

Winter is white like snowdrops gleaming in the sky.
Winter sounds like Father Christmas with his reindeers.
Winter smells like freezing-cold snow.
Winter looks like ice all over the ground.
Winter feels like really, really cold ice.
Winter tastes like freezing snow.

Liam Harlow (7)
The Grove Primary School, Cambridge

Winter

Winter looks like a lump of snow when nobody has walked on it.
Winter is cold like the sea.
Winter is red like burning leaves.
Winter sounds like a lovely cold snowball hitting my face.
Winter feels like a really cold ice went through my gloves.
Winter tastes like me eating a lot of snow.

Adam Thomas (7)
The Grove Primary School, Cambridge

Autumn

Autumn is green like our Year 3 tree.
Autumn sounds like a tune in the morning.
Autumn smells like bonfire sticks.
Autumn looks like me playing football at school.
Autumn feels like a soft teddy.
Autumn tastes like a big chocolate cake.

Hollie Dean (7)
The Grove Primary School, Cambridge

Summer

Summer sounds like blackbirds singing in the sky.
Summer smells like yellow flowers smelling fresh.
Summer looks like a massive orange tree.
Summer feels like a hot cup of tea at night.
Summer tastes like a burger in a frying pan.

Stacey Matthews (8)
The Grove Primary School, Cambridge

Friendship

Friendship is blue like my dark jumper.
Friendship sounds like little girls laughing in the woods.
Friendship smells like children spraying perfume in the lounge.
Friendship looks like five children making friends.
Friendship feels like people stroking my head while I am asleep.
Friendship tastes like juicy apples.

Danniella Willday (7)
The Grove Primary School, Cambridge

Autumn

Autumn is brown like the leaves trod on underfoot.
Autumn smells like the cold air in a gust.
Autumn sounds like the crunchy leaves in the autumn morning.
Autumn looks like me getting a nice hot drink.
Autumn feels like the cold material getting colder and colder.
Autumn tastes like the big meals that I eat on autumn days.

Alexander Scott (7)
The Grove Primary School, Cambridge

Autumn

Autumn is red like the leaves.
Autumn sounds like the birds singing in the morning
Autumn smells like a big chocolate cake.
Autumn looks like the orange leaves.
Autumn feels like rough leaves.
Autumn tastes like the fresh air.

Jack Goode (7)
The Grove Primary School, Cambridge

Autumn

Autumn is brown like the crunchy leaves.
Autumn sounds like the wild wind getting stronger.
Autumn smells like the fresh air in the morning.
Autumn looks like the white, cold, frosty morning.
Autumn feels like a bumpy, wet leaf.
Autumn tastes like a large chocolate cake

Jade Holmes (7)
The Grove Primary School, Cambridge

Summer

Summer sounds like the wind blowing.
Summer smells like a juicy apple on a tree.
Summer looks like the sun shining on my arms.
Summer feels like the hot sun shining.
Summer tastes like the fresh air.

Louis Cook (7)
The Grove Primary School, Cambridge

Summer

Summer is blue like a big, blue sea.
Summer sounds like big blue tit singing.
Summer smells like a giant strawberry.
Summer looks like the big, hot sun.

James Champion (7)
The Grove Primary School, Cambridge

Winter

Winter is blue like the sky.
Winter sounds like frozen icebergs.
Winter smells like fresh air.
Winter looks like a rainbow.
Winter tastes like a rotten apple.
Winter feels like the sea.

Liam Cassidy (7)
The Grove Primary School, Cambridge

Anger

Anger is black like a wolf.
Anger sounds like a bear roaring.
Anger looks like someone getting eaten by a fox.
Anger feels like getting bitten by a dog.
Anger tastes like gravy everywhere on my plate.

Kieran Peat (7)
The Grove Primary School, Cambridge

Summer

Summer is yellow like the sun shining in the morning.
Summer sounds like the birds singing in the morning sunshine.
Summer smells like a hot biscuit in the sky.
Summer looks like a rainbow.

Selena Russel (7)
The Grove Primary School, Cambridge

Summer

Summer is yellow like the shining sun in the afternoon sky.
Summer sounds like the singing birds in the morning.
Summer smells like sweet, juicy strawberries.
Summer looks like someone happy and smiling in the street.
Summer feels like a soft, creamy puppy.
Summer tastes like sweet pears picked off a tree.

Sabine Khabiri (7)
The Grove Primary School, Cambridge

Sadness

Sadness is blue like my broken robot.
Sadness sounds like my mum crying when I annoy her.
Sadness smells like smoke and fire when somebody's dying.
Sadness looks like somebody hitting and smacking you.
Sadness feels like when two people like each other
But they don't like you.
Sadness tastes like chicken kebabs.

Kalem Hart (7)
The Grove Primary School, Cambridge